The Complete Guide to Puggles

Vanessa Richie

LP Media Inc. Publishing
Text copyright © 2021 by LP Media Inc.
All rights reserved.

No part of this book may be reproduced or transmitted in any form or by any means, electronic or mechanical, including photocopying, recording, or by an information storage and retrieval system – except by a reviewer who may quote brief passages in a review to be printed in a magazine or newspaper – without permission in writing from the publisher. For information address LP Media Inc. Publishing, 3178 253rd Ave. NW, Isanti, MN 55040

www.lpmedia.org

Publication Data

Vanessa Richie

The Complete Guide to Puggles – First edition.

Summary: "Successfully raising a Puggle Dog from puppy to old age" – Provided by publisher.

ISBN: 978-1-954288-12-6

[1. Puggles – Non-Fiction] I. Title.

This book has been written with the published intent to provide accurate and authoritative information in regard to the subject matter included. While every reasonable precaution has been taken in preparation of this book the author and publisher expressly disclaim responsibility for any errors, omissions, or adverse effects arising from the use or application of the information contained inside. The techniques and suggestions are to be used at the reader's discretion and are not to be considered a substitute for professional veterinary care. If you suspect a medical problem with your dog, consult your veterinarian.

Design by Sorin Rădulescu

First paperback edition, 2021

Cover Photo Courtesy of Kacy Reece

TABLE OF CONTENTS

INTRODUCTION 2

CHAPTER 1

Breed History and Characteristics of the Puggle 3
Pugs – Mischievous Charmers 4
Beagles – Friendly, Joyful Charmers 7
A Few Decades Worth of Puggle History 8

CHAPTER 2

Puggle Attributes and Temperament 9
A Unique Looking Dog 10
    Pug Appearance 10
    Beagle Appearance 12
The Likely Temperament of the Puggle 13
    Pug Temperament 13
    Beagle Temperament 15
    Predicting the Puggle Temperament 16

CHAPTER 3

Is the Puggle Right for You? 17
  A Quick Word about Designer Dogs 20
Adult Versus Puppy 21
    Bringing Home an Adult Puggle 22
    Bringing Home a Puggle Puppy 23

CHAPTER 4

Finding Your Puggle **25**
A Word of Advice 26
Rescuing a Puggle 27
Choosing a Breeder 29
    Contracts and Guarantees 31
    Health Tests and Certifications 32
    Selecting a Puppy from a Breeder 33

CHAPTER 5

Planning for Your New Puggle **35**
Planning the First Year's Budget 36
Instructing Your Children 38
    Always Be Gentle and Respectful 38
    Mealtime 39
    Chase 39
    Paws on the Ground 39
    Keep Valuables Out of Reach 41
Preparing Your Current Dogs and Cats 41
    Stick to a Schedule 41
    Helping Your Dog Prepare – Extra at Home Playdates ... 44

CHAPTER 6

Preparing Your Home and Schedule **45**
Creating a Safe Space for Your Dog or Puppy 46
Crates 47
Puppy-Proof/Dog-Proof the House 48
    Plant Dangers 48
    Indoor Hazards and Fixes 49
    Outdoor Hazards and Fixes 51
Choosing Your Veterinarian 52

CHAPTER 7

Bringing Your Puggle Home — 55
Final Preparations and Planning — 56
    Ensure You Have Food and Other Supplies on Hand — 56
    Design a Tentative Puppy Schedule — 56
    Do a Quick Final Puppy-Readiness Inspection Before the Puppy Arrives — 58
    Initial meeting — 58
Picking up Your Puppy or Dog and the Ride Home — 59
The First Vet Visit and What to Expect — 61
Crate and Other Preliminary Training — 62
First Night Frights — 64

CHAPTER 8

The Multi-Pet Household — 65
Introducing Your New Puppy to Your Other Pets — 66
Introducing an Adult Dog to Other Pets — 68
Older Dogs and Your Puggle — 69
Dog Aggression and Territorial Behavior — 70
Natural Prey Drive — 71
Feeding Time Practices — 72

CHAPTER 9

The First Few Weeks — 73
Setting the Rules and Sticking to Them — 74
Establish a No Jumping and No Mouthing Policy — 75
    Nipping — 75
    Chewing — 75
    Jumping — 78
Attention Seeking and Barking — 78
Reward-Based Training Versus Discipline-Based Training — 80
Separation Anxiety in Dogs and Puppies — 80
How Long Is Too Long to Be Left Home Alone? — 81
Don't Overdo It – Physically or Mentally — 82

CHAPTER 10

Housetraining 83
Inside or Outside – Housetraining Options and Considerations 86
   Setting a Schedule 86
   Choosing a Location 88
   Keyword Training 88
Reward Good Behavior with Positive Reinforcement 89
Cleaning Up 89

CHAPTER 11

Socialization 91
Greeting New People 92
Greeting New Dogs 93
The Importance of Continuing Socialization 94
Socializing an Adult Dog 94

CHAPTER 12

Training Your Puggle 97
Benefits of Proper Training 98
Choosing the Right Reward 100
Name Recognition 100
Essential Commands 102
   Sit 103
   Down 103
   Stay 103
   Come 104
   Leave It 105
   Drop It 106
   Off 107
   Quiet 107
Where to Go from Here 108
   Puppy Classes 108
   Obedience Training 109

CHAPTER 13

Nutrition — 111
- Why a Healthy Diet is Important — 112
- Dangerous Foods — 113
- Canine Nutrition — 114
  - Proteins and Amino Acids — 115
  - Fat and Fatty Acids — 116
  - Carbohydrates and Cooked Foods — 116
- Different Dietary Requirements for Different Life Stages — 116
  - Puppy Food — 117
  - Adult Dog Food — 117
  - Senior Dog Food — 118
- Your Dog's Meal Options — 118
  - Commercial Food — 118
  - Homemade Diet — 121
- Scheduling Meals — 122
- Food Allergies and Intolerance — 122

CHAPTER 14

Playtime and Exercise — 125
- Exercise Needs — 126
- Outdoor Activities — 126
  - Chase — 126
  - Tricks – for Fun! — 127
  - Great Walking Companion — 128
  - Water Activities — 129
  - Dog Parks — 129
- Indoor Activities — 129
  - Hide and Seek — 129
  - Pillow and Blanket Forts — 130
  - Ice Cube Escape! — 130
  - Laser Pointers — 130
  - Puzzle Toys! — 130

What to Avoid	131
Activities That Could Hurt Their Backs	131
Leaving Them Alone Outside	131
Off Leash	131

CHAPTER 15

Grooming – Productive Bonding — 133

Grooming Tools	133
Coat Management	136
Puppies	136
Adult Dogs	136
Senior Dogs	138
Allergies	138
Bath Time	138
Cleaning Eyes and Ears	140
Trimming Nails	141
Oral Health	142
Brushing Your Dog's Teeth	142
Dental Chews	143

CHAPTER 16

General Health Issues: Allergies, Parasites, and Vaccinations — 145

The Role of Your Veterinarian	146
Allergies	146
Inhalant and Environmental Allergies	148
Contact Allergies	148
Fleas and Ticks	149
Parasitic Worms	151
Heartworms	152
Intestinal Worms: Hookworms, Roundworms, Tapeworms, and Whipworms	153
Vaccinating Your Puggle	155
Holistic Alternatives	156

CHAPTER 17
Genetic Health Concerns Common to the Puggle **157**
Common Pug Health Issues 158
    Skin Issues 158
    Allergies 158
    Brachial Issues 159
    Eye Problems 160
    Ear Problems 161
    Tail Problems 161
    Stomach Issues 162
    Encephalitis 162
    Intervertebral Disk Disease 162
    Legg-Calve-Perthes Disease 163
    Patellar Luxation 163
    Dental Issues – Small Mouths 163
    Anal Glands 165
    Obesity 165
Common Beagle Health Issues 165
    Dental Issues 165
    Allergies 165
    Back Problems 166
    Eye Problems 166
    Hemophilia 167
    Neurologic Issues 167
    Liver Disorder 167
    Heart Disease 168
    Cushing's Disease 168
    Hip Dysplasia 168
    Amyloidosis 170
    Obesity 170
Common Owner Mistakes 170
Prevention and Monitoring 170

CHAPTER 18

The Aging Puggle ... **171**
Senior Care Challenges – Common Physical Disorders
Related to Aging ... 173
Vet Visits - The Importance of Regular Vet Visits and
What to Expect ... 175
Changes That Might Occur ... 176
    Appetite and Nutritional Requirements ... 176
    Exercise ... 177
    Aging and the Senses ... 178
Keeping Your Senior Dog Mentally Active ... 178
Advantages to the Senior Years ... 179
Preparing to Say Goodbye ... 179
Grief and Healing ... 181

INTRODUCTION

The adorable-looking Puggle is a designer breed, with the parent breeds being the Pug and the Beagle. Puggles are an older designer breed, and they are popular because both parent breeds are a smaller breed of dog and incredibly different from most of the other breeds. They are fantastic companions that love to play and give you those puppy dog eyes for attention, treats, or just because they can.

Puggles typically have snouts that are slightly longer than that of the Pug, but they are still considered a brachial (short-nosed) breed. Since the parent breeds are so incredibly different looking, about the only guaranteed part of a Puggle's appearance is size. Considered a medium-sized dog, they are usually between 13 to 15 inches tall and weigh between 18 to 30 pounds.

There are a lot of differences in the personalities of the Pug and the Beagle, but what they share is that loving, gregarious nature that makes them so endearing. You might end up with a lazy lap dog or a high-energy outdoor champion. However, your Puggle is almost guaranteed to love playing with you – performing tricks, taking walks, playing outdoor games, or lounging around. Beagles are more independent, particularly compared to the Pug, but both breeds are incredibly loyal. Often the Beagle's natural curiosity and independent nature is tempered by the Pug's desire to stay close and clown around with the pack.

If you get the best of both worlds, you'll end up with a Puggle that loves to do tricks, play with you, and is enthusiastic about everything you want to do. In the worst-case scenario, you'll have a stubborn, uncooperative dog that may not be interested in listening to you. Either way, the dog is nearly certain to love you, but the way that affection is expressed will be different.

Be very careful about selecting a breeder. Since this is a popular designer breed, there are a high number of puppy mills and less ethical breeders who don't take the kind of care required to ensure that the parents have healthy puppies. And both the Pug and the Beagle have some serious health concerns, as well as a lot of less serious ones. You'll need to be careful about where you get your newest family member.

Whatever appearance and temperament your puppy has, you will have a great companion for you and your family. Puggles tend to love children, and they are robust dogs that can keep up with younger and older kids. As long as you keep an eye on the kids, everyone can have a great time.

CHAPTER 1
Breed History and Characteristics of the Puggle

Puggles are the result of two very different-looking dogs with diverse personalities. Apart from being incredibly friendly, you cannot be certain of how your Puggle will act. There is a very good reason for the very different personalities – the breeds have very different histories. Pugs have largely been companions, while Beagles have traditionally been very effective work dogs.

Photo Courtesy of Kacy Reece

CHAPTER 1   Breed History and Characteristics of the Puggle

Photo Courtesy of Mike Caprarola

Pugs – Mischievous Charmers

The earliest record of Pugs living with people dates back to 200 BC. They were introduced into Chinese culture during the Han dynasty, which lasted from 206 BC to 200 AD. It did not take long for this adorable little dog to go from being a new breed to a favorite of the most powerful people in China – the emperors and empresses.

One of the most intriguing features of the Pug – its very wrinkly face – has always been part of the breed's charm. It makes them look older, wiser, and more distinguished. This is somewhat in contrast to their large, cartoonish eyes.

The combination of Puggles' size and personality made them fantastic companions, so they were adopted into the homes of the Chinese emperors. The Pug became part of the family, not as a worker, as was the case for most dogs adopted by many other monarchs. Pugs lounged with emperors, empresses, and their families. They were not expected to do anything apart from distracting and entertaining the family. While some monarchs used their hounds for hunting and other sports, the Pug was never expected to do much of anything besides be present.

FUN FACT: Beagle Mom, Pug Dad

A Puggle is an adorable mix between a Pug and Beagle, but did you know that a Puggle's mother is almost always a Beagle? This is primarily because there are health risks associated with breeding a larger male dog with a smaller female.

Some people believe that the wrinkles were actually part of the breeding. The Chinese wanted more than just wrinkles; they wanted their dogs to have a more profound statement, literally on their faces. To some, the wrinkles look like the Chinese symbol for luck, which, if true, has worked as much to be good luck for the Pug as for their people.

This largely peaceful cohabitation between the Pug and China's ruling families played a large role in the development of the breed's personality. They were so favored that some of the families had guards for their Pugs. The breed remained popular in Asia for a very long time, but their popularity really exploded across the world toward the end of the 1500s when trade between Asia and Europe became more common. While exchanging and trading a wide range of goods, Europeans were impressed by how personable the Pugs were. Around this time, the first Pug made the trip to Europe with a Dutch trader, and the breed was called Mopshond. The Dutch still use this name today for the breed.

Just as they had a meteoric rise in China, the breed gained the attention of royalty in Europe. The Pug was a large part of family life for many royal families. Legend has it that Prince William of Orange was saved when his Pug warned him that the Spanish were advancing. As a result, Pugs were named the official dog of the House of Orange. The prince later became William III of England, and his family brought their Pugs with them from Holland to England.

Marie Antoinette had a Pug before her ill-fated marriage to Louis XVI. Following her execution and the rise of Napoleon, another Pug became prominent as the pet of Josephine Bonaparte.

Pugs were reintroduced into Europe from China later, giving the line a new infusion of genes. Though it was a much more hostile introduction (the British invaded the Chinese Imperial Palace and took Pugs from the royal families in 1860), it benefited the Pugs that were already in Europe.

Pugs made their way to the U.S. around this time. As the American Civil War ended, Pugs provided a welcome note of positivity, although they were not nearly as popular until more recently.

CHAPTER 1   Breed History and Characteristics of the Puggle

Photo Courtesy
of Jennifer Yates
Rainbowland Puggles

Beagles – Friendly, Joyful Charmers

Beagles are the preferred breed for fox hunting. Their loud baying voices make it easy to find them, and their enthusiasm for the chase is palpable. That enthusiasm comes from a very long history of working with people, and the desire to be active and working still remains in the breed.

Beagles have worked with humans for longer than their history has been recorded. No one knows for sure how long they have been instrumental in hunting and interacting with people. Even the origins of the name "Beagle" aren't entirely known. There are two popular theories about how the breed got its name.

1. Some point to the Gaelic word "beag," which means little, as the term from which the name is derived.

Photo Courtesy of Ryan Cooper

2. Others point to the French "be'geule," which is an onomatopoeic word to describe the baying of a hound.

Both of these terms could be an accurate way of describing different aspects of the dog, though it isn't known where the first examples of the breed were born. The dogs have long been associated with British fox hunting, and some of the earliest appearances of the dog in written history occur in England before the Roman invasion in 55 BC. According to the records, the British claim the breed as "the foothound of our country, indigenous to the soil." Early Beagles were small hardworking dogs that helped hunt hares and rabbits around the island. If this is true, it does seem more likely that the name derives from the Gaelic term, though it could be a combination of the two terms, particularly considering the long relationship between France and the British Isles.

By the 16th century, Beagles were a favorite of British royalty and the gentry. Like today, the nobility accumulated large packs of Beagles for tracking hares and rabbits and packs of larger hounds for hunting deer. The smaller dogs that chased hares with skill and enthusiasm were the ancestors of the breed we know today as Beagles. Beagle predecessors gained popularity because people with lesser means who couldn't afford to have a horse were still able to hunt with the smaller breed of dog. Older people who were no longer able to ride horses for hours could go for quicker excursions near home. Beagles were the perfect dog for hunting on foot, making them ideal for a much wider range of situations than larger hounds. They became popular on the continent, spreading the popularity of the Beagle far beyond the Isle.

Beagles arrived in the U.S. following the end of the Civil War. Given how important hunting was across much of the country, the Beagle was an immediate hit, helping people to survive across the large stretches of land. The American Kennel Club officially recognized the first Beagle in 1885, a dog named Blunder. Centuries of participating in the hunt means that Beagles are an intelligent, energetic breed, making them an ideal companion for more active people.

A Few Decades Worth of Puggle History

The first Puggle was bred during the 1980s. It took nearly two decades before the breed was made available commercially, with the first Puggles being sold during 2000. Since then, the Puggle has become incredibly popular with a wide range of people.

The American Kennel Club does not recognize designer dogs, but Puggles have been added to the American Canine Hybrid Club.

CHAPTER 2
Puggle Attributes and Temperament

With the Pug and Beagle having such completely different appearances, trying to predict how your Puggle will look is about as easy as predicting ten years into the future. Apart from their size and coat length, there isn't too much that these two breeds have in common in terms of their appearance.

Photo Courtesy of Stephanie Donovan

CHAPTER 2   Puggle Attributes and Temperament

A Unique Looking Dog

Both parent breeds have a unique look that makes it easy to identify them. With such a wide range of adorable potential looks, your Puggle is bound to be cute.

Pug Appearance

Pugs have a very distinctive look that makes them nearly impossible to confuse with any other breed of dog. Their appearance is one of the two things that make people love the Pug; the other is their incredibly charming personality. As a dog that adores people, they are easy to bring into any home. However, with a dog that has been immensely popular for so long, you have to be very careful about the breeder that you get the puppy from. There are some relatively universal personality traits, but Pugs also come in a very wide range of personalities, depending on their ancestors. This chapter looks at the universal characteristics and shared history of Pugs and Beagles.

One of the most intriguing features of the Pug – its very wrinkly face – has always been part of the breed's quirky charm. This contrasts with the large, protuberant eyes and wrinkled face and body.

Their lovely coats usually come in fawn and black. There are some Pugs with silver, white, and reddish colors, but they are usually mixed with the fawn color.

Pugs are a small breed with short hair and a very muscular body. The average weight of the Pug is between 13 and 18 pounds. Pugs have a lot in common with the stereotypical idea of what a dog should look like but on a small scale. It's absolutely adorable to watch those compact little frames scurrying to keep up with you – and your Pug will try to keep up as long as you are walking. The Pug is really a lap dog that wants to cuddle up with you and eat anything and everything you are willing to share. But those small frames cannot take a lot of extra weight, so you will need to make sure that you keep treats to a minimum and exercise your dog daily.

The two most noticeable features of the Pug are the face and the tail. Some people say that Pugs have humanoid faces, which is kind of true when you consider that most dogs have snouts that jut out quite a ways. Their tails are also adorable and unmistakable with the swirly curl up over the back.

Look at a Pug's face, and you will notice the flat nose, cartoonish eyes, and wrinkles. The eyes look like they take up about a third of the face, making Pugs look more like a cartoon dog than an actual dog. The wrinkles give them an interesting dignity that does not match their clownish personalities. Even people who think that Pugs are ugly find that they typically cannot resist cuddling these dogs and learn to love those distinctive faces. The coloring on their faces is also very easy to recognize. The ears and face are usually black, while the rest of their body is a lighter color. As they age, the black turns to grey, sometimes making them look like they have spectacles when the greying occurs around the very large eyes.

Their tails are very similar to the tails of pigs and bulldogs—cute little swirly tails that look more like springs than tails. It is endearing how that face and tail just wiggle when you walk in the door, making it nearly impossible not to cuddle your Pug as soon as you set eyes on him.

Photo Courtesy of Jen Jossie

Beagle Appearance

Beagles are easy to identify because of their popularity and the length of time they have been popular. Snoopy in the comic strip Peanuts is a Beagle. Those floppy ears framing an adorable, attentive face with a brown and black spotted coat just make the heart melt.

They are considered medium-sized dogs, but they are definitely on the smaller end, weighing between 20 and 35 pounds and averaging between 13 and 15 inches tall.

The vast majority of Beagles are tricolored, a white coat with black and brown patches. Beagles with two colors are called lemon Beagles, and they tend to have patches of unique colors, including tan, lemon, red, and chocolate. There are some that have a blue tricolor, but that is incredibly rare. Under that beautiful coat is a second coat – it's why Beagles are notorious shedders. The fur is considered medium-length, but it is the double coat that makes the little furballs so common in any home with a Beagle.

Though not quite as distinctive as the Pug's, the Beagle's face is very memorable. Their muzzles are long and rectangular, which fits well in their long skulls. The long floppy ears tend to hide the fact that their skulls are longer than the average dog skull in relation to the size of the dog. Then there are those large, dark eyes. Beagles are considered sighthounds, so those big eyes have a practical use (they aren't just there to make you feel guilty when you are eating food that you won't share).

Beagles have a very straight tail that they hold upright when they are excited or are focused on something. Their hind legs are angled and muscular. Their chests are large to hold the larger lungs required for the kind of running the working dogs have done in the past.

FUN FACT
Breed Popularity

Puggles originated in the 1980s and became one of the most popular hybrid breeds in the early 2000s. Still very popular companion dogs, Puggles are rated 207th most popular (out of 623 breeds) by polling website Dogell.com.

The Likely Temperament of the Puggle

"Since the Beagle has a high prey drive and was initially bred for rabbit hunting, the Puggle can have some of these characteristics (scent tracking, alarm barking, and determination). Pugs are affectionate, loyal, and sometimes stubborn. Families need to understand that their Puggle puppy might have a combination of both."

JENNIFER YATES
Rainbowland Puggles

Your Puggle's temperament, mental acuity, willingness to listen, and energy levels can vary wildly depending on which parent the pup takes after.

Pug Temperament

The Pug is an adaptable breed, in large part because of how much they love living with people. They will do nearly anything to make sure that you love to have them around and are cuddling up to them.

Most people with Pugs will tell you that they are loveable, charming, and loyal. About half of Pug owners will say that they are fairly easy to train; the other half will tell you that Pugs are incredibly stubborn. Whether or not your Pug is inclined to learning the rules, he is going to want to make you laugh and have fun. If you don't want to spend much time training your little friend, that will be perfectly fine with your Pug. What your Pug wants more than anything is to be a part of the family, to be included, and to follow you everywhere.

Pugs are not a breed that does well when left alone. For example, they may go a little crazy when left in a strange place alone, breaking vases and other items in the rooms.

Some Pugs are fairly quiet, beyond their very noisy snoring, and others are barkers. You will want to find out which type the parents are from the breeder to get an idea of whether your puppy is likely to be loud or quiet.

If you love to hike, your Pug will enjoy it too. If you like going to the park, your Pug will be more than happy to join you. If you are more of a couch potato, that will be perfectly acceptable too. This means that your Pug will easily adapt to your moods and won't be too upset with rainy days at home or with a day out and about. This makes them great travel companions or lounge about pooches.

CHAPTER 2   Puggle Attributes and Temperament

Pugs also tend to be very gentle, which makes them great for families with young kids. You will need to pay a lot more attention to how your child treats the Pug than how the Pug treats your child. Make sure that your kids are not too rough and don't squeeze the Pug. Your Pug will very likely be more patient than anyone could expect, but you don't want your adorable little pal to be hurt because of his patience with people.

Since Pugs are a breed that adores food, you really cannot leave any food lying around that your Pug can reach. Putting chocolates on the counter is almost certain to result in an unplanned emergency trip to see the vet. Food you leave on the coffee table probably is not going to be there when you get back. They may love you, but they also love food. Unlike dogs such as labs and golden retrievers that will appear incredibly remorseful for their wrongdoing, Pugs are much more likely to pretend that they didn't do anything wrong. The more stubborn your Pug, the harder it will be to get him to stop these kinds of actions.

Some breeders will go so far as to say that Pugs are the clowns of the canine world just because of how much they love attention. If it will make you laugh, they are willing to do virtually anything. Since they were bred to be with people, they are very aware of how you feel, and they want you to be happy. This makes them very enjoyable to be with at the end of a long or difficult day.

Photo Courtesy of Dotty Haake

Beagle Temperament

When it comes to people, Beagles are lovable, intelligent, gentle, and generally good-natured. They tend to be a bit warier of people and dogs they don't know, but they aren't prone to being particularly aggressive. If you are looking for a guard dog, the Beagle is not a good choice because any wariness they exhibit doesn't tend to last long. They tend to want to be friends, so they are just as likely to follow an intruder around your home if that intruder is nice to them – and even more so if the intruder gives them treats. They can be decent alarm dogs, though, since they usually have a healthy set of lungs and a voice that will wake up everyone in the home.

As a hound, they have an amazing sense of smell that they have learned how to put to good use to find anything that interests them. While this has historically been a great asset in finding hares, rabbits, and foxes, companion Beagles are far more likely to use their noses to find treats around your home.

This incredible sense of smell is coupled with a sharp intellect that will help them to do things that you didn't know dogs could do. For example, if you keep your trash in a cabinet that isn't locked, your Beagle will be able to smell when there is something potentially tasty and will likely be able to figure out how to get to it. This will mean child-proofing your kitchen (especially the pantry and trashcans) and the bathroom. Outside, Beagles may not only react to scents but to movements as well. Learning to keep them in check outside can be particularly trying as they are a lot stronger than you may think.

Photo Courtesy of Kari Hess

With their determination, you will have your work cut out for you with getting a Beagle to listen. If your dog's bark takes after the Beagle, you'll find out just how unique your dog's voice is compared to most dogs. Known as baying, the sound that Beagles make is quite intimidating because it is loud and low. When properly trained, you could get them to bay when they hear something going on outside to alert you.

Given how much Beagles love food, they can be easier to train than dogs like the Shiba Inu, but Beagles are still generally classified as a dog that is difficult to train. Short training sessions work best, especially with a lot of praise and a minimal number of treats (you don't want them to get too accustomed to treats and refuse to do what you say if food isn't involved).

Beagles are high energy, so they require either a lot of walking or frequent bouts of play to expend that energy. If you don't, they could escape your yard (they are phenomenal diggers) or find other ways to get around fencing. They are not a dog for homebodies, which is why they are a great companion for people who enjoy hiking or jogging. Since they love people, you can have your children help to tire out your dog (and your dog can help to tire your children). They also tend to love other dogs and cats (especially the litter box that comes with cats), so you can find other ways to help use up some of that energy.

Even though they are more independent than Pugs, Beagles are still very much a pack-oriented dog. Like Pugs, Beagles can suffer from separation anxiety, making it a bad idea to leave them home alone for long periods. Having other dogs around can help reduce that anxiety, but it is best not to leave them home alone for more than a few hours. Because Beagles are intelligent dogs, you really don't want to find out what they can get into or what they can destroy when they are anxious.

Predicting the Puggle Temperament

The Puggle is popular because, regardless of appearance, they combine some of the best temperaments of the parent dogs; they are affectionate, fun-loving, and typically intelligent. They enjoy playing with pretty much anyone, and being the center of attention is likely to be something that your Puggle excels in. Beyond this, the Puggle temperament is a wild card.

CHAPTER 3
Is the Puggle Right for You?

Now that you have a bit of knowledge about the history of the parent breeds, their appearance, and temperament, it's time to determine if the Puggle is the right dog for your home. They may be great dogs, but they really aren't for everyone, especially if you are looking for a more predictable temperament.

Photo Courtesy of Marinna Cammarn

CHAPTER 3   Is the Puggle Right for You?

The following provides a quick guide to help you determine if this is the right breed for you.

Element	Description
What's Great About Them	
A Fantastic First Family Dog	If you have never had a dog before, the Puggle is a fantastic dog for the first-time dog owner. From their gregarious nature to the ease of grooming, it is a great dog to have your family learn how to take care of a dog.
Easy to Exercise	Even if your Puggle takes after the Beagle parent, they aren't so large that exercising them is difficult. Chapter 14 details how long you should exercise your Puggle and some great activities to tire out your pup, but it is typically easy to do without consuming a large part of your day.
Good Watch Dog, but not a Good Guard Dog	The sounds that a Puggle makes are nearly impossible to ignore, so they can let you know that someone is outside your home before anyone knocks on the door. Their gregarious nature means they won't be attacking visitors, but it also means they aren't going to be a problem for intruders once an intruder makes it through the door.
Why They May Not Be Right for You	
Separation Anxiety	If you aren't home for much of the day, a Puggle probably isn't the right dog for you. If you don't have other dogs or if you will be gone for more than 8 hours a day often, this is not the breed for you.
Potential to Overheat	Brachial (short-snouted) dogs tend to overheat because dogs don't have sweat glands, so they cool off by panting. The shorter snout means that panting is a lot less effective. Your Puggle shouldn't be outside when it is particularly hot, and jogging isn't a good idea for any brachial dog. You will need to monitor your dog for signs of heat stress and must ensure he is well hydrated.

Not a Jogging Companion	This is another potential problem – if your Puggle has a face more like a Pug, you really can't jog with your pup. If you specifically need a jogging companion, you will want to find a different breed to be your newest family member.
Drooling, Snoring, and Snuffling	Brachial dogs tend to be noisy. You can hear them breathing in whichever room they are in. They drool a lot and tend to make a pretty big mess when they eat and drink. The noise and the mess that are a part of having a brachial dog can be incredibly frustrating to some people, and there isn't anything that your dog can do about it. If your dog has a short snout, you'll have to learn to live with the noises that come with that adorable face.
Inevitability of Shedding	For those with allergies or who want a breed that isn't prone to shedding, the Puggle is probably not going to be a good fit. Most of the year, they will have light to moderate shedding, but there will be several times a year when they will be prolific shedders. Chapter 15 provides details about grooming, so if you want to learn more about what you will need to do, jump ahead to see if the solution will fit your schedule.
Potentially Stubborn	If you are looking for a dog that is great at doing tricks or is easy to train, know that a lot of Puggle families say they are not easy to train. Others do find their Puggles to be a breeze in training. However, there is no guarantee on how much time it will take to train your dog.
Potentially Vocal	If you want a quiet dog, you are taking a risk in getting a Puggle. You have about as good a chance of your dog being vocal as your dog being quiet. Chapter 12 provides details on how to train a dog not to bark as much, though it is more effective for puppies than dogs that are already habitual barkers.

CHAPTER 3 Is the Puggle Right for You?

A Quick Word about Designer Dogs

While many designer dogs are bred for looks alone, the American Kennel Club advocates for pure breeds with longer histories and established temperaments, particularly those breeds that have declined in numbers, such as Otterhounds. The AKC's argument is that it is unnecessary for people to intentionally create a new breed of dog because many established breeds have the same sought-after traits through normal selective breeding. It is easier to predict the potential risks and problems of a single breed of dog than it is to establish a consistent new breed by crossing two different varieties of dogs.

As will be covered in a later chapter, looking into the parents' health and history is just as important for designer dogs as it is for purebred dogs. You should find a breeder who knows the parents well and who takes good care of both parents. Learning the parentage gives you an accurate idea of what your puppy's temperament and health will be.

Photo Courtesy of Lauren Mastrocola

Adult Versus Puppy

The final question to ask yourself before you settle on a breed is whether you should get an adult or a puppy. With a breed like the Puggle, it will be harder to find an adult than a puppy—but not impossible.

There are a lot of positives and negatives with both, and ultimately, the answer varies based on the individual or family. Here are some considerations to help you determine which age is a better fit for your home.

Photo Courtesy of Kacy Reece

CHAPTER 3 Is the Puggle Right for You?

Bringing Home an Adult Puggle

With a breed like a Puggle, you need to be careful about adopting an adult; if the dog is not properly trained, life can turn into a real struggle. Adopting an older Puggle can require a lot of work, so knowing the dog's history is very important in order to prepare for the dog's behavior.

Puggles can be stubborn, and an adult might also be a bit wary, especially if he hasn't been socialized or was previously treated poorly. If you have young children at home, you will need to make sure to watch your dog closely and make sure he has a positive reaction to kids before bringing him home, especially if you don't know the dog's history with children. You will also need to be careful about introducing a Puggle to other pets, though most Puggles tend to warm up to other animals fairly quickly.

On the positive side, older dogs can give you more immediate gratification. You don't have to go through the sleepless nights that come with a new puppy. The odds are also that you aren't going to be starting from scratch with housetraining.

Additionally, adult dogs are awake during the day more than puppies, and while it may take your dog a bit longer to warm up to you, you can bond much faster with an adult.

Finally, one of the biggest benefits of acquiring an adult dog is that it will already be its full size. There is no need for guessing how big your dog will grow, and that makes it far easier to purchase the appropriate-sized gear and supplies right from the start.

The following is a list of questions to consider when adopting an adult Puggle:

- **Can you properly dog-proof your home before the dog arrives?**

You can't simply bring a dog into your home, whether an adult or a puppy, and let him run around unchecked. To be sure he learns the rules of the house before roaming freely, you will need to have a safe, dedicated space for your new dog. (Details of how to dog-proof your home are discussed in Chapter 5.)

- **Do you have pets who will be affected by a new dog?**

Puggles are likely to get along just fine with any dog – and probably cats – but you will still want to be very careful since you don't know the dog's history with other animals. This introduction should take place over the first couple of months. Introducing the animals in a neutral territory will show you what to expect when your Puggle and your current dogs are together on a permanent basis. Even if they appear to be compatible, you still need to keep them apart for a while. This will ensure your new Puggle understands that other

FUN FACT
Puggles on the Silver Screen

Puggles gained some extra notoriety with the 2019 Netflix series, It's Bruno! The comedy, set in Bushwick, Brooklyn, features a man and his Puggle named Bruno. Bruno's owner is played by Solvan Naim, while Bruno is played by his real-life dog named Bruno! The series was nominated for Outstanding Short-Form Comedy or Drama Series at the 71st Primetime Creative Arts Emmy Awards in 2019.

dogs are part of the pack and are not a threat to him.

You will need to be aware of how your other dog(s) reacts as well. Even if your current dog is very friendly, you will still want to be careful when introducing the two and allowing them to interact in your home.

- **What is the dog's health history?**

A complete health record for a rescue Puggle may not be available, but it is likely you will find a dog that has already been spayed or neutered as well as chipped. Unless you adopt a Puggle with health issues, which should be disclosed by the rescue organization if known, rescues tend to be less costly than puppies at their first vet visit. In other words, for the first few years, your Puggle's health care visits should not be too expensive.

Bringing Home a Puggle Puppy

Puppies are a major time investment, and a dog as intelligent and potentially stubborn as the Puggle will make some aspects of raising a puppy that much harder. How much time can you devote to a puppy's care? Will you be able to deal with an excitable puppy that has everything to learn?

A puppy will be a better fit if you put in dedicated time for training and socializing before the dog becomes set in his ways. If you have other pets at home, a puppy is definitely a better choice than an adult because he is young and can be trained to follow YOUR rules. (The exception would be if you find an adult that is already well-socialized.)

The following should be considered when determining whether or not a Puggle puppy is a good fit for your home:

- **How much time do you have available for training and socialization?**

All puppies are a lot of work, starting with the moment the puppy enters your care. While the Puggle's temperament is not very predictable, how you train and socialize your puppy will affect every aspect of the dog's adult life. Training and socializing can take up a large chunk of time in the beginning, but both are absolutely essential for raising a healthy Puggle.

CHAPTER 3 Is the Puggle Right for You?

- **Are you able to show firmness and consistency when training such an adorable puppy?**

From the very beginning, you have to establish yourself and your family as the ones in charge; your Puggle must understand his place in the family hierarchy. You will need to be patient and consistent with your training, no matter how frustrated you become or how cute those puppy eyes appear. All intelligent dogs have a streak of stubbornness!

- **Do you have the time, energy, and budget to puppy-proof your home?**

The preparation of your home for your puppy's arrival begins long before he first sets foot in your house. Puppy-proofing your home is as time-consuming as child-proofing your home. If you do not have the time for this, then you should consider getting an adult dog instead of a puppy. (Details of how to puppy-proof your home are discussed in Chapter 5.)

What most people love about adopting a puppy is that they will spend more time with a puppy than with an adult dog since the puppy still has its whole life ahead of it. You will receive records about the puppy and the puppy's parents, which will make it easier to identify any problems your Puggle might experience in the future. This makes it considerably easier to keep your puppy healthy and to spot potential issues before they become major problems.

Some people find it easier to bond with puppies than with adult dogs. A young puppy may be nervous in a new home, but most adjust quickly because they are predisposed to enjoying the company of those around them.

Photo Courtesy of Vinny Parrish

CHAPTER 4
Finding Your Puggle

By this point, you are probably quite excited about your Puggle. You should know if you want a puppy or an adult, as well as have a basic understanding of what you need to avoid to get a healthy, happy Puggle. Now it's time to find the right dog for your home.

Photo Courtesy of Jane Mccafferty

CHAPTER 4 Finding Your Puggle

A Word of Advice

Pet stores should generally be avoided for purchasing any breed, but particularly a designer breed that is as popular as the Puggle. Pet stores and puppy mills typically don't pay attention to good breeding habits. Many problems can arise at the beginning of a puppy's life from inappropriate conditions and treatment during the mother's pregnancy and the first few weeks of life. To ensure you find a healthy puppy to be your loving companion for as long as possible, you must find a reputable breeder who cares about his dogs.

Do your research before bringing your Puggle home.

The average lifespan of a Puggle is between 10 and 15 years. You will want to have as much protection as possible against genetic ailments, especially since both parent breeds are fairly older breeds; this means finding a breeder who always puts the puppies' health first.

Unlike purebred dogs, potential genetic problems for the Puggle come from two different breeds; luckily, both breeds are fairly well-documented when it comes to health concerns. (Details are discussed in Chapter 17.) You should learn the medical history of the puppy's parents to ensure your puppy has the best chance of living a healthy, happy life.

If you adopt an older dog, it will be much harder to know about the breeding history. You will need to spend more time paying attention to your dog and learn about the potential health problems (Chapter 17) associated with both breeds so that you can see the early warning signs as early as possible.

> **FUN FACT**
> **American Canine Hybrid Club (ACHC)**
>
> Hybrid dog breeds can't be registered with the American Kennel Club (AKC) because they aren't purebred breeds, but there are other options for keeping track of hybrid dog ancestry. The American Canine Hybrid Club (ACHC) is an online registry for hybrid dog breeds and was established in 1969. Their registry indexes over 700 hybrid breeds! The purpose of registration is to keep track of ancestry and parentage so that when you purchase an ACHC-registered dog, you know exactly what its ancestry looks like. The ACHC recognizes all hybrids who are produced from two purebred breeds, including Puggles. The first Puggle was registered with the ACHC by a Wisconsin dog breeder named Wallace Havens. For more information, visit www.achclub.com.

Rescuing a Puggle

There are a surprisingly high number of rescues for Puggles, in part because of the length of time they have been around. The following are a few websites dedicated to helping people find a Puggle for their home, as well as a few rescue groups that may have Puggles and Pugs up for adoption:

- Puggles Rule
- Welcome to Pacific Pug Rescue
- Puggle Dogs for Adoption in USA
- Operation Paws for Homes (not Puggle specific)

Instead of searching for rescue organizations, you might want to rescue a Puggle from a breeder. They will have a better understanding of the dog and its personality, and they will be able to answer any future questions you might have.

Keep in mind the following questions when adopting a Puggle:

- What is the reason the dog was surrendered?
- Did the dog have any health issues when he arrived?
- Do they know how the dog was treated by the previous family?
- (What kind of training was he given, was he mistreated, and was he socialized?)
- How many homes has the dog experienced?
- What kind of veterinary care did the dog receive? Are there records that confirm this?
- Will the dog require extra medical attention based on known or suspected problems?
- Is the dog housetrained?
- How well does the dog react to strangers while walking in unfamiliar areas?
- Does the dog have good eating habits, or does he tend to be more aggressive when eating?
- How does the dog react to children and to other dogs and pets?
- Does he have any known allergies?
- Does the dog have any known dietary restrictions?
- If there are problems with the dog after adoption, will the organization take him back?

CHAPTER 4 Finding Your Puggle

Rescue groups should have at least a basic understanding of how the Puggle interacts with other dogs.

It is unlikely that you will find a Puggle at a shelter. Shelters are rarely certain of the breeds of dogs because their charges are often abandoned, dropped off, or rescued without any information on genetics.

Photo Courtesy of Emily Correa

Choosing a Breeder

Finding a responsible breeder is the best thing you can do for your puppy because good breeders work only with healthy Pug, Beagle, and Puggle parents, which reduces the odds of serious health issues.

Always take the time to do your research before moving forward. You can start with breeders in surrounding areas in your state, or you can start researching sites that are strictly dedicated to the breed. Although breeders for Puggles are largely reputable, you also might run across an individual who is more interested in making a lot of money than in caring for his dogs.

The goal is to locate breeders who are willing to answer ALL of your questions patiently and thoroughly. They should show as much love for their Puggles as they expect you to show for your new puppy; their goal should be to locate good homes for all of their animals.

It is a particularly good sign if you find a breeder who posts pictures and information about the dog's parents, documents the progress of the mother's pregnancy, and shares descriptions of all vet visits. The best breeders will also stay in contact with you and answer any questions that might arise after you take the puppy home. These are also breeders who are likely to have waiting lists. Taking an active interest in what happens to the puppies in their new home shows that they care a great deal about each individual dog.

You also want to find a breeder who is willing to talk about problems that might develop with your Puggle. Good breeders will ensure the adopting family is capable of properly socializing and training their Puggle since both of these activities are essential as a puppy matures.

It is likely that your conversation with each breeder will last about an hour. If a breeder does not have time to talk when you call and isn't willing to call you back—cross them off your list! Also, after you have talked with each possible breeder, take the time to compare their answers to your questions and make sure you take careful notes during every interview.

The following are some questions to consider when researching breeders:

- Ask if you can visit in person. The answer should always be yes, and if it isn't, you don't need to ask anything further. Thank the breeder and hang up. Even if the breeder is located in a different state, they should always allow you to visit their facility.
- Ask about the required health tests and certifications they have for their puppies. (These points are detailed further in the next section, so make sure to check off the available tests and certifications with every breeder.) If they don't have all of the tests and certifications, remove the breeder from your list of considerations.

CHAPTER 4 Finding Your Puggle

- Make sure the breeder takes care of the initial health requirements, particularly shots, for each puppy—from the first few weeks of birth through the dog's early months. Puppies require certain procedures before they leave their mother in order to ensure they are healthy. Vaccinations and worming typically start at around six weeks of age

Photo Courtesy of Sue Vidinovski

and should be continued every three weeks. By the time your puppy is old enough to come home with you, he should be well into the first phase of these procedures or completely finished with these important health care needs.

- Ask if the puppy is required to be spayed or neutered before reaching a certain age.
- Question whether or not the breeder is part of a Puggle organization or group.
- Ask about the first phases of your puppy's life, such as how the breeder will care for the puppy prior to its going home with you. They should be able to provide a lot of details, and they should not sound irritated by your questioning. They should also explain what training your puppy will receive prior to leaving the facility. It is possible the breeder might start house training your puppy. If so, ask about the puppy's progress, so you know where to pick up training once your Puggle reaches your home.
- The breeder should be more than happy to help guide you in doing what is best for your dog because they should want their puppies to live happy, healthy lives. You should also be able to rely on any recommendations your breeder makes about taking your puppy home, particularly about the first days with the puppy.
- Ask how many varieties of dogs the breeder manages in one year and how many sets of parents he owns. Mother dogs should have some downtime between pregnancies before producing another litter. Learn about the breeder's standard operations to be sure they take care of the parents and treat them like valuable family members—not strictly as a way to make money.
- Ask about aggression in the puppy's parents and find out if there are other dogs in the breeder's home. While a puppy's temperament is more malleable than an adult's, some exposure to other breeds might make it easier when integrating him into a home that already has dogs.

Contracts and Guarantees

Breeder contracts and guarantees are meant to protect the puppies as much as they are meant to protect you. If a breeder has a contract, make sure you read through it completely and are willing to meet all of the requirements prior to signing. Contracts tend to be fairly easy to understand and to comply with, but you should be aware of all the facts before you agree to anything. Signing the contract indicates you are serious about committing to giving your puppy the best care possible and to meeting the minimum care requirements set forth by the breeder.

A contract may state the breeder will retain the puppy's original registration papers, although you will receive a copy of the papers, too.

If a family does not meet all requirements as stated in the contract, it is the breeder's responsibility to remove that puppy from the family. These are the dogs some breeders offer for adoption.

A guarantee states the kind of health care the breeder's puppy is to receive once it leaves the breeder's facility. This typically includes details about the dog's current health and the recommendations for the next steps in the puppy's health care. Guarantees may also provide veterinary schedules to ensure that the health care started by the breeder is continued by the new puppy parent. In the event that a major health concern surfaces, the puppy will be returned to the breeder.

The contract will also explain what is not covered by the guarantee. A guarantee tends to be quite long (sometimes longer than the contract), and you should also read it thoroughly before the signing.

Puggle contracts usually include a requirement that the dog be spayed or neutered once it reaches maturity (typically six months). The contract may also contain requirements for naming your puppy (designer breeds are not as likely to have this requirement since they are not registered; if you would like more information about naming requirements, check out the American Kennel Club for details about contracts), details of the puppy's health, and a stipulation regarding what will happen if you can no longer take care of the animal. (The dog is usually returned to the breeder.) Information concerning the steps that will be taken if the new owner is negligent or abusive to the dog is also included in the contract.

Health Tests and Certifications

A healthy puppy requires healthy parents and a clean genetic history, which is a bit more difficult to guarantee in a Puggle due to the brief history of this breed. A breed with so many potential genetic issues, like the Puggle, needs a breeder who seriously follows good breeding practices. A conscientious breeder keeps extensive records for each puppy and its parents. You should review each of the parents' complete histories to understand what traits your puppy is likely to inherit. Pay attention to temperament, learning traits, attachment issues, and any other personality traits you consider important. You can request these documents be sent to you electronically, or you can pick them up when you visit the breeder in person.

It might be time-consuming to review the breeder's information for each parent, but it is always well worth the time. The more you know about the parents, the better prepared you will be for your puppy.

All breeders should ensure their Pugs undergo the following health tests:
- Hip Evaluation
- Ophthalmologist Evaluation
- Patella Evaluation
- Pug Dog Encephalitis DNA Test

All breeders should ensure their Beagles undergo the following health tests:
- Hip Evaluation
- Ophthalmologist Evaluation
- Musladin-Lueke Syndrome (MLS) DNA Test (test for a genetic mutation that causes MLS)

Selecting a Puppy from a Breeder

Selecting your puppy should be done in person. However, if the breeder is willing to share videos and pictures, you can start checking out your puppy immediately after he is born!

You should consider the following steps once you are allowed to visit the puppy in person:

- Assess the group of puppies as a whole. If most or all of the puppies are aggressive or fearful, this is an indication of a problem with the litter or (more likely) the breeder. The following are considered red flags if they are displayed by a majority of the puppies:
    - Tucked tails
    - Shrinking away from people
    - Whimpering when people get close
    - Constant attacking of your hands or feet (beyond pouncing)
- Notice how each puppy plays with the other puppies in the litter. This is a great indicator of how your puppy will react to any pets you already have at home.
- Notice which puppies greet you first and which puppies hang back to observe you from afar.
- Puppies should not be over or underweight. A swollen stomach is generally a sign of worms or other health problems.
- Puppies should have straight, sturdy legs. Splayed legs can be a sign that there is something wrong.

CHAPTER 4   Finding Your Puggle

- Examine the puppy's ears for mites, which will cause a discharge if present. The inside of the ear should be pink, not red or inflamed.
- The eyes should be clear and bright.
- Check the puppy's mouth for pink, healthy-looking gums.
- Pet the puppy to check his coat for the following:
    - Be sure the coat feels thick and full. If the breeder has allowed the fur to get matted or dirty, it is an indication they are likely not taking proper care of the animals.
    - Check for fleas and mites by running your hand from the head to the tail; then check under the tail as fleas are more likely to hide under a dog's tail. If mites are present, they may look like dandruff.
- Check the puppy's rump for redness and sores; try to check the puppy's last bowel movement to ensure its firmness.

Pick the puppy that exhibits the personality traits you want in your dog. If you want a forward, friendly, excitable dog, the first puppy to greet you may be the one you choose. If you want a dog that will think things through and let others get more attention, look for a puppy that sits back and observes before approaching you.

CHAPTER 5
Planning for Your New Puggle

Given how different the intellects between the two parent breeds are, it will be best to prepare your home for an intelligent dog – and that means some extra work. Intelligent dogs can break into things, putting the dog more on the level of a toddler. To ensure that your Puggle doesn't get into your cabinets, trash cans, and other areas where he shouldn't go, you are going to need to plan well ahead of your pup's arrival.

Photo Courtesy of Brooke Lindy

CHAPTER 5   Planning for Your New Puggle

Planning the First Year's Budget

Whether you get a puppy or an adult dog, the costs are always higher than you initially think, or even the second or third thought. You will definitely want a budget, which is a good reason to start purchasing supplies a few months in advance. When you buy the items you need, you will begin to formulate an idea of how much money you will spend each month. Many of these items are one-time purchases (or won't need to be bought too often, like a bed), but many other items, like food and treats, will have to be purchased regularly.

The following table will help you plan your budget. Keep in mind the prices are rough estimates and may be significantly different based on your location.

Item	Considerations	Estimated Costs
Crate	You may need two crates: one for the puppy and one for when the puppy grows up unless the dog will remain small. This should be a comfortable space where the puppy will sleep and rest.	Wire crate: $60 to $350 Portable crate: $35 to $200
Bed	You may need two beds: one for the puppy and one for when the pup grows up. This will be placed in the crate.	$10 to $55
Leash	It should be short in the beginning because you need to be able to keep your puppy from getting overly excited and running to the end of a long line.	Short leash: $6 to $15 Retractable: $8 to $25
Doggie bags for walks	If you walk at dog parks, this won't be necessary. For those who don't have daily access to bags, it is best to purchase packs to ensure you don't run out.	Singles cost less than $1 each. Packs: $4 to $16
Collar	You may need two collars: one for a puppy and one for an adult Puggle.	$10 to $30

Tags	These will likely be provided by your vet. Find out what information the vet provides for tags; then, purchase any tags that are not provided. At a minimum, your Puggle should have a tag with your address on it in case the pup escapes.	Contact your vet before purchasing to see if the required rabies tags include your contact info.
Puppy food	The larger the bag of dog food, the higher the cost, but the fewer times you will need to purchase food. You will need to purchase specific puppy food in the beginning. Adult dog food is more expensive.	$9 to $90 per bag
Water and food bowls	These will need to be kept in the puppy's area. If you have other dogs, you will need separate bowls for the puppy.	$10 to $40
Toothbrush/ Toothpaste	You will need to brush your Puggle's teeth regularly, so plan to buy more than one toothbrush during the first year.	$2.50 to $14
Hairbrush	Puggle coats are incredibly easy to maintain, but you should still brush them regularly. When they are puppies, brushing offers a fantastic way to bond.	$3.50 to $20
Toys	You definitely want to get toys for your puppy; you will want toys for more aggressive chewers (separation anxiety can make your Puggle an aggressive chewer when you are gone), especially if your puppy goes through them quickly. Also, buy your adult Puggle toys.	$2.00 Packs of toys range from $10 to $20 (which is easier in the long run as your pup will chew through toys quickly)
Training treats	You will need treats from the beginning, and likely won't need to change the treats based on your Puggle's age; you may need to change treats to keep your dog's interest, however.	$4.50 to $15

CHAPTER 5   Planning for Your New Puggle

You will need to pay attention to when items need to be replaced based on your dog's size. Ultimately, you need to establish a budget for the initial costs; then create a second budget for items that will need to be replaced. Plan to revisit this list at the end of every year so you can make sure your dog remains comfortable and happy.

Instructing Your Children

In order to make your puppy feel comfortable in its new home, you must make sure your children are careful and gentle with the dog, whether you adopt a puppy or an adult dog. Since Puggles look like living stuffed animals, some kids may try to treat the puppy like a toy, which could be detrimental to your dog. You should make sure your children follow all of the "puppy rules" from the very beginning to ensure your puppy feels safe, happy, and isn't accidentally injured.

The following are the Five Golden Rules your children should follow from day one. They apply both to puppies and adult Puggles:

1. Always be gentle and respectful.
2. Do not disturb the puppy during mealtime.
3. Chase is an outside game.
4. The Puggle should always remain firmly on the ground. Never pick him up.
5. All valuables should be kept out of the puppy's reach.

Since your kids are going to ask why these rules are necessary, the following are some explanations you can use. If necessary, modify the discussion to meet the audience—what you say to a toddler is a lot different than what you should tell a teen about playing with your Puggle.

Always Be Gentle and Respectful

Little Puggle puppies are ridiculously cute and cuddly, but they are also more fragile than adult dogs. At no time should anyone play roughly with a puppy. It is important to be respectful of your puppy to help him learn to also be respectful toward people and other animals.

This rule must be applied consistently every time your children play with your puppy. Be firm if you see your children getting too excited or rough. You don't want the puppy to get overly excited either because he might end up nipping or biting someone. If he does, it won't be his fault because he is still learning as a puppy. Make sure your children understand the possible repercussions if they get too rough.

HELPFUL TIP
Children Pet Safety Tips

Puggles are excellent companion dogs and have a reputation for being good with kids, but it's always a good idea to familiarize your kids with a few dog safety tips before bringing your new dog home. Here are some suggestions for rules to discuss as a family:
- Don't pull on the dog's ears or tail.
- Never approach the dog suddenly, especially when it is eating.
- Never hit or yell at the dog.

With adequate supervision and early socialization, your Puggle will fit right in with the family in no time.

Mealtime

Puggles can be protective of their food, especially if you rescue a dog that has previously had to fend for himself. Even if you have a puppy, you don't want it to feel insecure during his mealtime because it will learn to be aggressive whenever it eats. Save yourself, your family, and your dog from problems by making sure mealtime is your dog's time alone. Teach your children their own mealtime is off-limits to the puppy, as well.

No feeding your new dog from the table! From toddlers to teens, this is something you'll really need to emphasize—particularly for foods that your kids don't like. Puggles are pets, not garbage disposals, and no amount of cute puppy eyes should be rewarded with scraps from the table. That is a recipe for disaster as it will get harder to convince your dog to stop begging if other people aren't following your rules.

Chase

Make sure your children understand why a game of chase is perfect for the outdoors (though you'll need to monitor things), but inside the house, chase is off limits!

Running inside your home gives your Puggle puppy the impression your home isn't safe for him because he is being chased; it also teaches your puppy that running indoors is allowed, which can be dangerous as the dog gets older and bigger. One of the last things you want to see is your adult Puggle go barreling through your home—knocking into people and furniture—because it was fine for him to run in the house when he was a puppy!

Paws on the Ground

It doesn't matter if your Puggle looks like a stuffed animal—he is a living, breathing creature, and he needs to have his paws on the ground. Even though you might want to carry your new family member around or play with the pup like a baby, you and your family will have to resist that urge. The

CHAPTER 5 Planning for Your New Puggle

younger your children are, the more difficult it will be for them to understand the difference. It is so tempting to treat the puppy like a baby by carrying him around, but this is incredibly uncomfortable and unhealthy for the puppy.

Older children will quickly learn that a puppy's nip or bite hurts a lot more than one would think, and some Puggles do nip. Those little teeth are quite sharp, and if he nips at you, he could accidentally be dropped—no

Photo Courtesy of Jessica Monteserrato

one wants that to happen. If your children are never allowed to pick up the puppy, things will be a lot better for everyone involved. Remember, this also applies to you, so don't make things difficult by doing something you constantly tell your children not to do.

Keep Valuables Out of Reach

Valuables are not something that should end up in your puppy's mouth—whether they are toys, jewelry, or shoes. Your kids will be less than happy if their personal possessions are chewed up by an inquisitive puppy, so teach them to put toys, clothes, and other valuables far out of the puppy's reach.

Preparing Your Current Dogs and Cats

Puggles are equal-opportunity adorers—they love to love the people and dogs who live with them! You should start socializing them with your other dogs or pets when they are puppies. In most cases, this is a fairly straightforward process as long as your pets are comfortable with you bringing a puppy into their home.

The following are important tasks you should complete when preparing your current pets for the new arrival:

- Set a schedule for activities and the people who will need to participate.
- Preserve your current dog's favorite places and furniture; make sure your current dog's toys and other personal items are not in the puppy's space.
- Have playdates at your home to observe your dog(s) reactions to having an addition to the house.

Stick to a Schedule

It's essential to have a schedule. Obviously, the puppy is going to receive a lot of attention in the beginning, so you need to make a concerted effort to be sure your current pets know you will still care for them. Set a specific time in your schedule when you can show your current dog(s) how much you love them, and make sure you don't stray from that schedule after the puppy arrives.

When you bring the puppy home, plan to have at least one adult present for each dog you have in your home. If you have a cat in the home, the introduction will need to be slow and methodical, but Puggles tend to be fine with cats, especially if they are puppies and grow up with cats. If you bring home an adult Puggle, you will need to be careful and keep the dog and cat

CHAPTER 5 Planning for Your New Puggle

Photo Courtesy of Lauren Mastrocola

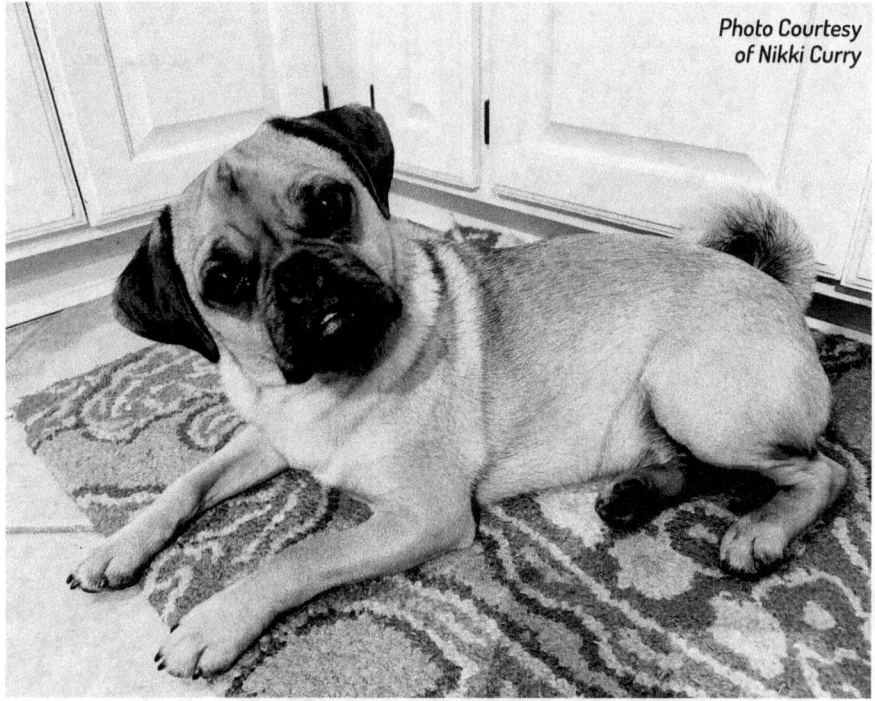

Photo Courtesy of Nikki Curry

separate when you aren't around to monitor them. Over time, it is likely they will learn to be fine with each other.

Having a schedule in place for your other dogs will make it easier to follow the plan with the puppy. Puggles love to be prepared for what is about to happen—at least in the beginning.

Once he has arrived, your puppy is going to eat, sleep, and spend most of the day and night in his assigned space. This means your puppy's space cannot block your current canine's favorite furniture, bed, or anywhere he rests during the day. None of your current dog's "stuff" should be in the puppy's area either; this includes toys. You don't want your dog to feel as if the puppy is taking over his territory. Make sure your children also understand to never put your current dog's things in the puppy's area!

Your dog and your puppy will need to be kept apart in the beginning (even if they seem friendly) until your puppy has received his vaccinations. Puppies are more susceptible to illness during these early days, so wait until the puppy is protected from possible diseases before the dogs spend time together. Leaving the puppy in his puppy space will keep them separated during this critical time.

CHAPTER 5   Planning for Your New Puggle

Helping Your Dog Prepare – Extra at Home Playdates

The following explains strategies that will help prepare your current pooch for the arrival of your puppy:

- Consider the personality of your dog to predict what might happen when the puppy arrives. If your current dog loves other dogs, this will probably hold true when the puppy shows up. If your current dog is territorial, you will need to be cautious when introducing the two dogs, at least until the Puggle has become part of the pack. Excitable dogs need special attention to keep from getting agitated when a new dog comes home. You don't want them to be so excited they make the Puggle feel threatened.

- Consider the times when unfamiliar dogs have been in your home. How did your current dog react to these other furry visitors? If your canine became territorial, be cautious when introducing your new pup. If you have never invited another dog into your home, organize a playdate with other dogs before your Puggle puppy arrives. You need to know how your current furry babies will react to new dogs in the house so you can properly prepare. Meeting a dog at home is quite different from encountering one outside the home.

- Think about your dog's interactions with other dogs for as long as you have known him. Has your dog shown protective or possessive behavior, either with you or others? Food is one of the reasons dogs will display aggression because they don't want anyone eating what is theirs. Some dogs can be protective of people and toys, too.

- If you know someone who owns a Puggle, Pug, or Beagle, organize a playdate so that your current dog becomes aware of the temperament of a Puggle.

These same rules apply, no matter how many dogs you have. Think about their individual personalities as well as how they interact together. Similar to humans, you may find when your dogs are together, they act differently. This is something you will need to keep in mind as you plan their first introduction. (Details of how to introduce your current dog(s) and your new puppy—plus how to juggle the two new personalities—are included in Chapter 9.)

CHAPTER 6
Preparing Your Home and Schedule

Preparing your home for a new puppy or dog is just as time-consuming as preparing for a toddler. Protecting your Puggle is the priority, and this will be a challenge if the dog has the same amazing sense of smell as the Beagle parent. You are going to spend a lot of time both inside or outside of your place preparing it for your newest family member. That clever little Puggle brain is going to start working out ways to get around barriers if you don't make sure to secure your new dog's designated area. Keep in mind, even an adult dog should be restricted in the beginning as he learns about your home and you learn more about his personality.

Even after you've completed the initial preparations, a weekly review leading up to your Puggle's arrival is necessary to make sure you don't miss anything and that everything is in place. Your new family member should have a safe space that includes all of the essentials. This will help to ease your new pup's mind and make the initial arrival a fun experience for everyone.

Whether bringing home a puppy or an adult, it is going to take time for your Puggle to learn to listen. Your new family member must learn that you are in control, and that could be a challenge if your Puggle is stubborn. Even after that, he may not want to listen to you all of the time. If your current dog already grabs food, climbs on furniture, and disregards your restrictions, training your new puppy will be difficult. Dog-proofing your home will help you keep your dog safe while he is learning to listen to you.

> **HELPFUL TIP**
> **Poison Control**
>
> Because Puggles are small, they might eventually get into something hazardous in your house that you thought was out of reach. Potential poisonous substances include certain plants, people foods, and household cleaners. If you think that your dog may have ingested something poisonous, your first line of defense before rushing to the vet could be the ASPCA Animal Poison Control Center hotline. This hotline is staffed 365 days a year, 24 hours a day, and can be reached at 888-426-4435. The ASPCA charges a fee for this service, to fund their organization. Before calling a hotline, make sure that your pet is safe, breathing, and acting normally. If your pet is exhibiting any strange symptoms, always make sure to contact your vet first.

CHAPTER 6 Preparing Your Home and Schedule

Photo Courtesy of Jennifer Yates Rainbowland Puggles

Creating a Safe Space for Your Dog or Puppy

Your puppy will need a dedicated space that includes a crate, food and water bowls, pee pads, and toys. All of these things need to be in the area where the puppy will stay when you are not able to give him attention. The puppy's space should be gated so your Puggle cannot get out and young children (or dogs) cannot get in. It should be a safe space where the puppy can see you going about your usual business and feel comfortable.

An adult will need a similar setup as a puppy, with all of the same items, but you can give the adult dog a bigger area. Pee pads may be necessary while the adult dog adjusts to his new environment, even if it is already house trained.

Crates

Crate training can be fairly easy (covered in Chapter 7), but not if you have a crate that is too big, too small, or too uncomfortable for your dog to feel like it is a safe place. To make training easier, be sure the puppy's crate and bedding are set up and ready before your puppy arrives.

Never treat the crate like it is a prison for your puppy. It's meant to be a safe haven after overstimulation or when it's time to sleep. Ensure your dog never associates the crate with punishment or negative emotions. The crate should be adjustable so you can make it a bit larger when your puppy becomes an adult—just in case your dog does end up on the larger end of the Puggle size. You can also get your puppy a carrying crate in the early days to make trips to the vet a little easier. A smaller crate will not work when your Puggle is an adult, but a carrying crate has plenty of space for a puppy.

As mentioned in an earlier chapter, a crate can be used to help with housetraining. The Puggle is one of the harder breeds to house train, which is not a welcome piece of news! You may want to have a pee pad in an area several feet away from the puppy's crate so he can go to the bathroom while keeping the area around his bed clean. Make sure to find out from the breeder if the puppy has already begun housetraining. If he is already making progress, you may not want to add the pee pad since that can be confusing to the puppy.

Photo Courtesy of Mike Caprarola

CHAPTER 6 Preparing Your Home and Schedule

Puppy-Proof/Dog-Proof the House

The most dangerous rooms and items in your home will be as dangerous to your puppy as if he were a little baby. The biggest difference is your Puggle is going to become mobile much faster than a child. He will get into dangerous situations immediately if you don't eliminate all the hazards before his arrival. Be aware that puppies will try to eat virtually anything! Nothing is safe—not even your furniture—and he will also gnaw on wood and metal. Anything within reach is considered fair game! Keep this in mind as you go about puppy-proofing your home.

Even if you bring home an adult dog, you will need to look for all of these dangers and make sure they are removed before your Puggle adult arrives.

Plant Dangers

You will need to be mindful of the plants in and around your home that could be hazardous to your dog. The following are thirty-four kinds of plants that should not be within your dog's reach. Remember to check both inside and outside your home.

Mildly Toxic	Mildly to Moderately Toxic	Moderately Toxic	Moderately to Highly Toxic	Highly Toxic
Asparagus Fern	Aloe	Alocasia	Cactus	Brunfelsia
Begonia	Amaryllis	Arrowhead	Kalanchoe	Desert Rose
Ficus Benjamina	Calla Lily	Dieffenbachia		Flame Lily
Flamingo Flower	Cyclamen	Dracaena Fragrans		Kaffir Lily
Gardenia	Dracaena	English Ivy		Oleander
Geranium	Philodendron	Eucalyptus		Sago Palm
Golden Pothos		Peyote		Bird of Paradise (Strelitzia)
Jade Plant				
Schefflera				
Ti Plant				
ZZ Plant				

Indoor Hazards and Fixes

This section explains where you should focus your dog-proofing attention inside your home. In case of problems, be sure your vet's number is posted on the fridge and in at least one other room in the house. Even if the number is programmed into your phone, family members or dog-sitters will still need to see the vet's number.

A Puggle will be an avid explorer, wanting to get into everything if given the opportunity. Get on your hands and knees and see each room from your Puggle's perspective—you will find at least one thing you missed previously.

Hazards	Fixes	Time Estimate
Kitchen		
Poisons	Keep in secure, childproof cabinets or on high shelves.	30 min.
Trash Cans	Use a lockable trash can or keep it in a secure location.	10 min.
Appliances	Make sure all cords are out of reach.	15 min.
Human Food	Keep out of reach.	Constant (Start making it a habit!)
Floors		
Slippery Surfaces	Put down rugs or special mats designed to stick to the floor.	30 min. – 1 hour
Training Area	Train on non-slip surfaces.	Constant
Bathrooms		
Toilet Brush	Either have one that locks into the container or keep it out of reach.	5 min./bathroom
Poisons	Keep in secure, childproof cabinets or on high shelves.	15 – 30 min./bathroom
Toilets	Keep lids closed. Do *not* use automatic toilet-cleaning chemicals.	Constant (Start making it a habit!)
Cabinets	Keep locked with childproof locks.	15 – 30 min./bathroom

CHAPTER 6   Preparing Your Home and Schedule

Laundry Room

Clothing	Store clean and dirty clothes off the floor and out of reach.	15 – 30 min.
Poisons (bleach, pods/detergent, dryer sheets, and misc. poisons)	Keep in secure, childproof cabinets or on high shelves.	15 min.

Around the Home

Plants	Keep off the floor.	45 min. – 1 hour
Trash Cans	Have a lockable trash can or keep it in a secure location.	10 – 30 min.
Electrical Cords/ Window Blind Cords	Hide cords or make sure they are out of reach; pay particular attention to entertainment and computer areas.	1 – 1.5 hours
Poisons	Check to make sure there aren't any in reach (WD40, window/screen cleaner, carpet cleaner, air fresheners); move all poisons to a central, locked location.	1 hour
Windows	Be sure cords are out of reach in all rooms.	1 – 2 hours
Fireplaces	Store cleaning supplies and tools where the puppy can't get into them; Cover the fireplace opening with something the puppy can't knock over.	10 min./fireplace
Stairs	Cordon off so that your puppy can't go up or down the stairs; make sure to test all puppy gates for safety.	10 – 15 min.
Coffee Tables/ End Tables/ Nightstands	Clear of dangerous objects (e.g., scissors, sewing equipment, pens, and pencils) and all valuables.	30 – 45 min.

If you have a cat, keep the litter box off the floor. It needs to be somewhere that your cat can easily get to it but your Puggle cannot. Since this involves training your cat, it's something you should do well in advance of the puppy's arrival. You don't want your cat to undergo too many significant changes all at once. The new canine in the house will be enough of a disruption! If your cat associates the change with your Puggle, you may find the feline refusing to use the litter box.

To get the litter box out of your dog's reach, you'll need to put it up high and preferably somewhere that doesn't have a chair that your dog can use. Clever pups can figure out how to get to places where you think they shouldn't be able to go.

Outdoor Hazards and Fixes

This section explains the areas that need your attention outside your home. Remember to also post the vet's number in one of the sheltered outdoor areas in case of an emergency.

Hazards	Fixes	Time Estimate
Garage		
Poisons	Keep in secure, childproof cabinets or on high shelves (e.g., car chemicals, cleaning supplies, paint, lawn care) – this includes fertilizer.	1 hour
Trash Bins	Keep them in a secure location.	5 min.
Tools (e.g., lawn, car, hardware, power tools)	Make sure all cords are kept out of reach and never hang over the side of surfaces.	30 min. – 1 hour
Equipment (e.g., sports, fishing)	Keep out of reach and never hang over the side of surfaces.	Constant (Start making it a habit!)
Sharp Implements	Keep out of reach and never hang over the side of surfaces.	30 min.
Bikes	Store off the ground or in a place the Puggle cannot get to (to keep the pup from biting the tires).	20 min.
Fencing (Can Be Done Concurrently)		
Breaks	Fix any breaks in the fencing. You need to make sure your Puggle can't easily get out of your yard.	30 min. – 1 hour

CHAPTER 6   Preparing Your Home and Schedule

Gaps	Fill any gaps, even if they are intentional, so your Puggle doesn't escape.	30 min. – 1 hour
Holes/Dips at Base	Fill any area that can be easily crawled under.	1 – 2 hours
Yard		
Poisons	Don't leave any poisons in the yard.	1 – 2 hours
Plants	Verify that low plants aren't poisonous; fence off anything that is (such as grapevines).	45 min. – 1 hour

If you have a pool, make sure it is secure so that your dog cannot get into it without your help. Covers may not always be enough (especially for intelligent breeds that may want to swim on their own terms), so make sure to have fencing or some other kind of deterrent to keep your Puggle safe. You always need to be particularly careful with brachial dogs because they have enough breathing issues already. Even if your dog loves swimming, you want to make sure you are always around when your dog is in the pool – especially if it is an accidental swim.

Never leave your Puggle alone in the garage, even when he is an adult. Your puppy will be in the garage when you take car trips, which is why it is important to puppy-proof this area.

As with the inside, you will need to check your outdoor preparations by getting down low and inspecting all areas from a puppy's perspective. Again, you are all but guaranteed to find at least one thing you missed.

Choosing Your Veterinarian

You should choose a vet before you bring your dog home because, as with any doctor appointment, scheduling a veterinary appointment may take a while. Vets that specialize in a particular breed are scarce, so it might be difficult to arrange the first appointment. Find a vet and book the first appointment well in advance of your dog's arrival.

Whether you bring home a puppy or an adult dog, your canine should see the vet within the first forty-eight hours of his arrival. This may be a requirement included in the contract with the breeder. Twenty-four hours is strongly recommended to make sure your dog is healthy. If there is a vet near you who specializes in or has worked with Puggles before, that will be best for your pup.

The following are some things to consider when looking for a vet:
- What is the vet's level of familiarity with Pugs and Beagles?
  The vet doesn't have to be a specialist, but a vet with experience with both of the parent breeds is helpful. As popular as the Puggle breed is, you can even ask if they have treated Puggles before. Even if the vet has

Photo Courtesy of Andy and Pam Warren

CHAPTER 6   Preparing Your Home and Schedule

only worked with one of the parent breeds, it is beneficial since they can help explain what to expect in the different stages of your dog's life.
- How far from your home is the vet?
- You don't want the vet to be more than thirty minutes away in case of an emergency.
- Is the vet available for emergencies after hours, or can they recommend a vet in case of an emergency?
- Is the vet part of a local veterinary hospital, or does the doctor refer patients to a local pet hospital?
- Is the vet one of several partners, or does he work alone? If he or she belongs to a partnership, can your dog see the same vet for all office visits?
- How are appointments booked?
- Can other services be performed at the clinic, such as grooming and boarding?
- Is the vet accredited?
- What is the price for the initial visit? What are the prevailing costs for routine visits that might include such things as shots?
- What tests and checks are performed during the initial visit?
- Can you visit the vet you are considering before you bring your dog home? If so, inspect the office environment and ask if you can speak to the vet. He or she should be willing to put you at ease and to answer your questions. Even though a vet's time is valuable, they should take a few minutes to help you feel confident about your decision to trust them with your new dog's health.

CHAPTER 7
Bringing Your Puggle Home

The first time a dog comes into the home is an incredibly exciting and memorable experience. Laughs are nearly guaranteed as your new family member begins a hesitant – or overly enthusiastic – exploration of the new place. Whether you bring home an adult or a puppy, you want to make the experience as pleasant and safe for your Puggle as possible. To have the best possible first introduction, you need to put a lot of time into planning and preparing for the main event.

This chapter covers how to introduce your new Puggle to your home. If you already have a dog, refer to Chapter 8 because you will need to introduce the animals outside of the home before your pup makes that grand entrance. Once you understand how to introduce dogs to each other, come back here to see how to introduce your new family member to your home and any family members who weren't able to make that initial meet and greet.

Puggles are famously friendly, but new experiences may be a bit overwhelming or scary for any dog. Make sure to make the environment as friendly as possible for your new pup and your people. This includes having a space dedicated for your new Puggle, even if you rescue an adult. If you have cats, keep them out of your new dog's space. You want to make sure to take it slow in the early days when introducing and socializing your new dog with other family members and pets so that your new addition isn't too overwhelmed.

Photo Courtesy of Sarelle Kiel

CHAPTER 7 Bringing Your Puggle Home

Photo Courtesy of Mike Caprarola

Final Preparations and Planning

Your new pup will almost certainly have separation anxiety, and there is a lot you can do to prepare for that, starting with taking time from work during the first twenty-four to forty-eight hours; the best-case scenario would have you at home for the first week or two. The more time you dedicate to helping your new little friend become accustomed to his surroundings, the better.

Ensure You Have Food and Other Supplies on Hand

The day before your Puggle arrives, review the list you created after Chapter 5 and do a quick check to ensure you have everything you need. Take a few moments to consider if there is anything you are missing. This will save you from having to rush out for additional supplies after the arrival of your new family member.

Design a Tentative Puppy Schedule

Prepare a tentative schedule to help you get started over the course of the first week. Your days are about to get remarkably busy, so you need somewhere to begin before your puppy arrives.

Photo Courtesy of Amy Fennell

CHAPTER 7   Bringing Your Puggle Home

The following are three key areas to establish before your puppy arrives:
- Feeding
- Training (including housetraining)
- Playing

When you bring home a puppy, you may be expecting a ball of high energy. However, puppies of any breed (no matter how active they will be later) sleep between eighteen and twenty hours per day. Having a predictable sleep schedule will help your puppy grow up healthier.

In the beginning, you won't need to worry about making sure that your puppy is tired out by the end of the day. His stamina will build fairly quickly, though; by the end of the first year, your pup will be a lot more active! As your pup starts to sleep less and play more, he will need thirty to sixty minutes of daily physical activity.

In the early days, your puppy's schedule will revolve around sleeping and eating—with some walking and socialization. Waking hours will include training and play.

Do a Quick Final Puppy-Readiness Inspection Before the Puppy Arrives

No matter how busy you are or how carefully you follow the puppy-proofing checklist, the day before your puppy arrives, be sure to set aside an hour or two to double-check that everything is in place.

Initial meeting

Review Chapter 5 rules with all of the family members the day of the dog's arrival and before the pup actually arrives. Place heavy emphasis on how to handle the Puggle, particularly the part about not picking up your newest family member. The puppy is already going to be in a state of shock, so don't compound that by literally taking the world out from under your Puggle's feet.

Determine who is going to be responsible for primary puppy care and for primary training. To teach younger children responsibility, a parent can pair with a child to manage the puppy's care. The child can be responsible for feeding the puppy and keeping the water bowl filled. Of course, a parent should oversee these tasks.

Picking up Your Puppy or Dog and the Ride Home

A good bit of planning and preparation goes into picking up your puppy, especially if you are going to the breeder's home. If possible, do this on a weekend or during a holiday weekend or season. This will allow you unrushed, quality time at home with your new puppy.

As tempting as it is to cuddle the puppy in your lap, it is both safer and more comfortable for the puppy if you use a crate for the ride home; two adults should also be present for the ride. This is the time to start teaching your puppy that car trips are enjoyable. This means making sure that the crate is securely anchored; you don't want the crate to slide around while he is helplessly sitting inside. This would be a terrifying experience for the puppy!

- The crate should be anchored in the car for safety and should include a cushion. If you have a long trip, bring food and water for the puppy and plan to stop at different intervals of the trip. Do not put food and water in the crate; sloshing water can scare your puppy. You can cover the bottom of the crate with a towel or pee pad in case of accidents.
- Call the breeder to make sure everything is still on schedule and make sure the puppy is ready to leave.
- Arrange for the mother dog to leave her scent on a blanket to help make the puppy's transition more comfortable.
- Make sure the second adult will be on time so that the two of you can head to the pick-up destination.
- If you have other dogs, make sure all of the adults involved in the introduction process know what to do. They should know the time and place for that first neutral territory meeting.

If you do not have other dogs, you can pick up your puppy and head straight home. If you have a trip that lasts more than a couple of hours, stop periodically so your puppy can stretch, exercise, drink, and use the bathroom. Keep your puppy away from other dogs until he has gotten all of his shots; you don't want him to be exposed to a dog that is carrying a disease against which your puppy is not fully protected.

At no point should your puppy be left alone in the car. If you have to use the restroom, either go before leaving the meetup place, or if you have a longer drive ahead of you, have at least one adult remain with the puppy during each stop.

If the puppy has never ridden in a car before, a second person should show the puppy attention while the other person drives. The puppy will be

CHAPTER 7 Bringing Your Puggle Home

in the crate, but someone can still provide comfort. The puppy will definitely be scared without his mom, siblings, or familiar people to console him. Having an adult present to talk to the puppy will make it less of an ordeal for the little guy.

When you arrive home, immediately take the puppy or dog outside to use the bathroom. Even if he had an accident in his crate, this is the time to start training your new family member to use the bathroom.

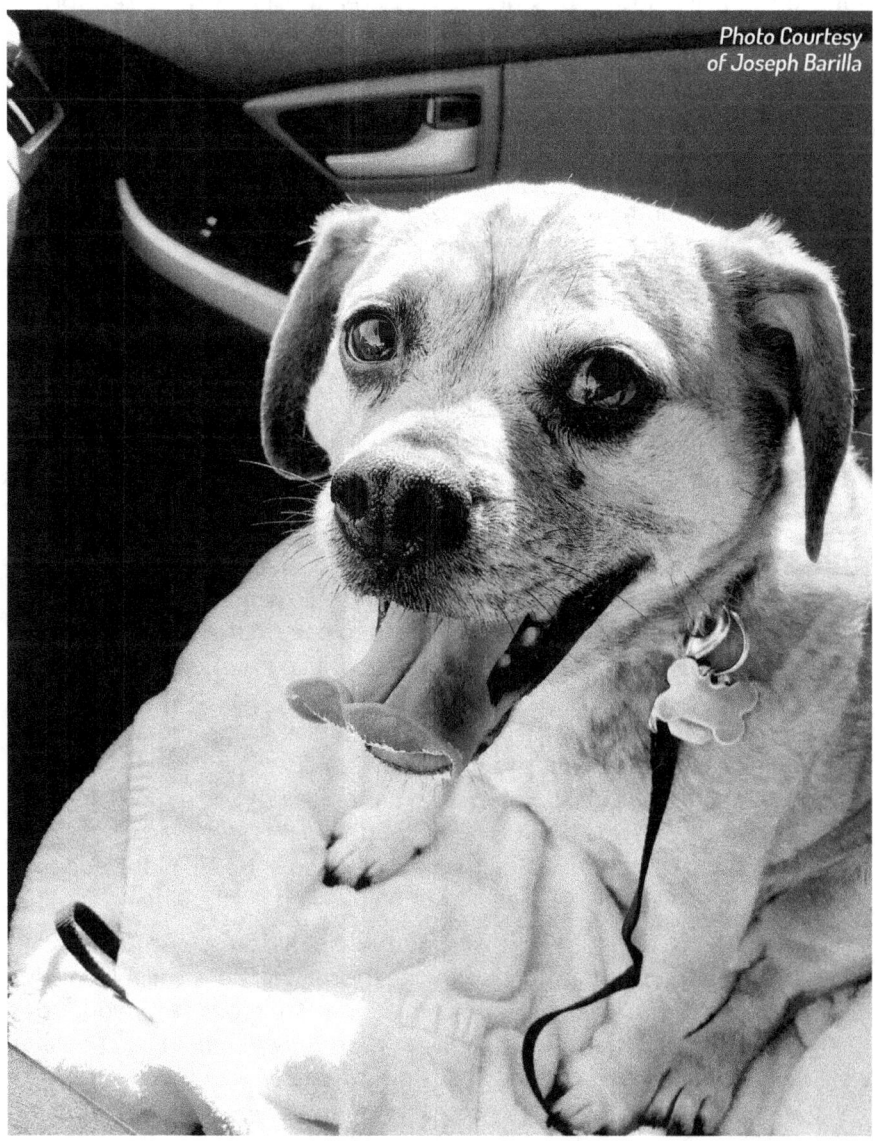

Photo Courtesy of Joseph Barilla

The First Vet Visit and What to Expect

A veterinary visit is necessary within the first two days of your puppy's arrival; in fact, it may be required in the contract with the breeder. Even if you bring home an adult dog, you should get to the vet within the first two days of your Puggle's arrival. The first visit will establish a baseline for the puppy's health. This will also allow the vet to track your puppy's progress and monitor his health as he grows. In addition to providing a chance to ask questions and get advice, this initial assessment will give you more information about your puppy. It also creates an important rapport between your Puggle and the vet.

During that first veterinary visit, your pup won't know what to expect. Try to ease his anxiety; you want this first appointment to set a positive tone for all future visits. This will likely be trickier with an adult than with a puppy, so be prepared to soothe any nervousness. As friendly as the breed tends to be, this is still a lot of changes in a very short period of time.

The following is a list of several things that must be completed before the day of the appointment:

- Find out how early you need to arrive to complete the paperwork for the new patient.
- Find out if you should bring a stool sample for that first visit. If so, collect it the morning of the visit and make sure to take it with you.
- Bring the paperwork provided by the breeder or rescue organization for the vet to add to your dog's records.

Upon your arrival, your Puggle may want to meet the other pups and people in the office. Although you will need to be mindful, this is an opportunity to socialize the puppy and to create a positive experience with the vet. Before letting your puppy meet other animals, always ask the owner for permission and wait for approval. Most pets at the vet's office are likely to not be feeling well, which means they may not be very affable. You don't want a grumpy, older dog or a sick animal to nip or scare your puppy. Negative social experiences are situations your puppy will remember; they could make a visit to the vet something to dread. Nor do you want your puppy to be exposed to potential illnesses before he has had all his shots.

During the first visit, the vet will conduct an initial assessment of your Puggle. One of the most important things the vet will do is weigh your dog or puppy. This is something you are going to have to monitor for your dog's entire life as you will want to ensure that your Puggle remains at a healthy weight. Keep a record of his weight so you can see how quickly your puppy is growing and to make sure you aren't overfeeding your dog. Ask your vet

CHAPTER 7 Bringing Your Puggle Home

what is considered a healthy weight for every growth stage and record that as well. Your Puggle puppy will be adult-sized by the end of the first year, so make sure your new pup reaches that size in a healthy amount of time—not gaining excessive weight over just a few months.

The vet will set a date for the next group of shots, which will likely happen not too long after the initial visit. After your Puggle receives his vaccinations (detailed in Chapter 16), prepare for a couple of days of your puppy feeling under the weather.

Crate and Other Preliminary Training

Contrary to what some people think, crates are a safe space for dogs. It is kind of like their own room. Even Puggles may want a little time on their own, and that is what their crate provides. For you, the crate is a place where your Puggle can stay safe, especially if he has separation anxiety. Your stuff and your dog are protected from any destructive tendencies. Crate training will prepare your dog for the occasion when you may have to board him, and he will be put in a crate if you ever travel on a plane.

Puppies younger than six months should not be left in a crate for hours at a time. Your Puggle will not be able to hold his bladder long, so you must make sure he has a way to get out and to go to the bathroom. If you adopt an adult Puggle that is not housetrained, you will need to follow the same rules. If you aren't sure about whether or not the dog is housetrained, it is best to treat the adult like a puppy until you are certain that your newest family member won't use the house as a bathroom.

Make sure the crate door is set so that it doesn't close on your dog during his initial sniff of the crate. You do not want your Puggle to be scared by the door as it is closing behind him; this could make him fearful of the crate in the future.

HELPFUL TIP
Great Crates for the Ride Home

Properly securing your dog in the car is important for your dog's safety and your own, but in the excitement of bringing home a new furry friend, especially one as small and sweet as a Puggle, it's easy to forget safety in favor of keeping your new puppy close. A great way to meet in the middle is to purchase a dog crate that can be buckled into your car, similar to the way a child's car seat might be secured. The crate will keep your puppy safe and out of your lap, where it can cause distraction and potential accidents. These crates are usually made of soft material with plenty of windows so that you can see your puppy and he can see you!

The following are some suggestions:

- Use a positive, cheerful voice as you let your Puggle sniff the crate for the first time. The first experience in the crate should be associated with excitement and positive emotions. Be sure your dog understands the crate is a good place. If you have a blanket from the puppy's mother, put it in the crate to help provide an extra sense of comfort.
- Drop a couple of treats into the crate if your canine seems reluctant to enter. Do NOT force your dog into the crate. If your dog refuses to go all the way inside the crate, that is perfectly fine. It has to be HIS decision to enter, so it doesn't become a negative experience.
- For a week or two, feed your dog while he is in the crate. Besides keeping the food away from any other pets, this will create positive associations between your Puggle and the crate.
    - If your dog appears comfortable with the crate, put the food all the way at the back.
    - If not, place the food bowl in the front; then, move it further back in the crate over time.
- Start closing the door once your dog appears to be eating comfortably in the crate. When the food is gone, open the crate door immediately.
- Leave the door closed for longer periods of time after your dog has finished eating. If your pup begins to whine, you know you have left your Puggle in the crate for too long.
- Crate your dog for longer periods of time once he shows no signs of discomfort in the crate when he is eating. Train him to go into the crate by simply saying, "Crate" or "Bed." Then, praise your dog and let him know that he has done an excellent job.

Repeat this for several weeks until your dog seems comfortable in his crate. The regular repetition several times a day teaches your dog that the crate is not a punishment and everything is alright. Initially, you should do this while you are still at home or when you go out to get the mail. When you leave the room, and your puppy lasts half an hour without whining, you can leave your pup alone for longer periods of time. However, keep this alone time to no more than an hour in the beginning.

During the first few weeks, you should begin to housetrain. Basic behavioral training is also vital from the start. However, you should let some time pass before taking your new puppy to structured training classes. Wait until he has all of his vaccinations. Knowledgeable trainers will not accept puppies in their classes until a dog's first full round of shots is complete.

Chapters 11 and 13 provide a closer look at how to train your dog.

First Night Frights

That first night is going to be terrifying for your little Puggle puppy! As understandable as this may be, there is only so much comfort you can give your new family member. The more you respond to cries and whimpering, the more he will learn negative behavior provides the desired results. You need to prepare for a balancing act—one that reassures the Puggle that he is safe while keeping him from associating crying with receiving attention from you.

Create a sleeping area for your puppy near where you sleep. The area should have the puppy's bed tucked safely into his crate. This will offer him a safe place to hide and a place where he will feel more comfortable in this strange new home. The entire area should be blocked off to be sure no one can get in (and the puppy can't get out) during the night. This sleeping area should also be close to where people sleep so that the puppy doesn't feel abandoned. If you were able to get a blanket or pillow that smells like the mother, make sure that this is in your puppy's space. Consider adding a little white noise (like an old-fashioned alarm clock) to cover unfamiliar sounds that could scare your new pet.

Your puppy will make noises over the course of the night. Don't move the puppy away, even if the whimpering keeps you awake. Being moved away from people will only scare the puppy more, reinforcing the anxiety he feels. When your puppy whines during the night, he is not whimpering because he's been in the crate too long. He's scared or wants someone to be with him—he's probably never been alone at night before coming to live with you. Spare yourself trouble later on by teaching the puppy that whimpering will not get him out of the crate. Over time, being close to you at night will be enough to reassure your puppy that everything will be fine.

In the beginning, puppies will need to go to the bathroom every two to three hours. This means you will also need to get up during the night! Make sure your puppy understands he must always go to the bathroom outside before bedtime or on the pee pad. If you ignore this rule, you will have a tough time training him to only relieve himself outside and not in the house.

If you choose to let your dog on the bed, wait until he is housetrained. Otherwise, you might have to replace your mattress within a short time. It is best to simply keep your Puggle off the furniture so he doesn't get hurt, and your furniture doesn't get ruined!

CHAPTER 8
The Multi-Pet Household

Puggles are an easy breed to bring into the home because most of them love other people and other dogs. They may be a little hesitant at first, but they tend to warm up quickly to everyone – it's why they aren't great at guarding your home. The younger a dog is when you start socialization, the more quickly they will feel comfortable with other dogs and pets.

It is actually best if you have at least one other dog so that your Puggle isn't home alone while you are shopping or at work. If you have a socialized adult dog, your current dog can also help teach your new Puggle the rules, and he could even become a mentor to your puppy. When your Puggle sees your dog listening to your commands, he will imitate this behavior, something that could be really helpful with a potentially stubborn breed. However, this works both ways. If your current dog displays negative behavior, you should try to correct these habits before your puppy arrives. You don't want your Puggle pup learning bad habits.

Photo Courtesy of Aleasha Barrus

CHAPTER 8 The Multi-Pet Household

Photo Courtesy of Kacy Reece

Puggles are typically good with cats, but you will still want to be very careful. They may want to play with the cat, and it is likely that if your cat runs, your dog will take that as a game of chase. For your cat's sake, make sure there is a consistently dog-free place for your cat to hide.

Introducing Your New Puppy to Your Other Pets

Introduce all new dogs to your current dog or dogs, regardless of age, in a neutral place away from your home. Even if you have never had problems with your current dog, you are about to change his world. When introducing your dog to the new puppy, select a park or other public area so your current dog will not feel territorial. This gives both animals the opportunity to meet and to become familiar with each other on neutral ground.

When introducing the two dogs, make sure you have at least one other adult with you so that there's one person for each canine. All dogs should be leashed so that you can quickly and easily move them apart if the introduction does not go well. If you have more than two dogs, then you should have one adult per dog. This will make it easier to keep all of the dogs under control. Even the best dogs can get excited about meeting a puppy. One of the people who needs to be at this meeting is the person who is in charge of the pets in your home. This helps establish the pack hierarchy.

Don't hold your puppy in your arms when the dogs meet. While you may want to protect the puppy, holding him has the opposite effect. Instead, your puppy will feel trapped, but if the puppy is on the ground, he can run if he feels scared. Stand near the puppy with your feet a little bit apart, so he can hide behind your legs if he decides he needs to escape.

All dogs should have a few minutes to sniff each other, making sure there is always some slack in each leash. This will help the dogs feel more relaxed, and they won't feel like you are trying to restrain them. Your dog will either want to play, or he might simply ignore the puppy. If the dogs want to play, be careful your current dog doesn't accidentally hurt the puppy, and if your dog ends up ignoring the puppy after an initial sniff, that is fine, too. If your dog is clearly unhappy, keep all of the dogs apart until everyone is comfortable with the meeting. Don't force the situation.

This introduction could take a while, depending on each individual dog's personality. The friendlier and more accepting your current dog is, the easier it will be to incorporate your new puppy into the home. For some dogs, a week is enough time to start feeling comfortable together. For other dogs, it could take a couple of months before they are fully accepting of a new puppy. Since this is a completely new dynamic for your dog, he may be angry with you for bringing this bundle of energy into his life.

The older your current dog, the more likely it is that a puppy will be an unwelcome addition. Older dogs can get cranky around a puppy that doesn't

Photo Courtesy of Eleonor Hughes

know when enough is enough! The goal is to make your puppy feel welcome and safe and to also let your older dog know that your love for him is as strong as ever.

Once your new family member and the rest of the canine pack become acquainted and comfortable, you can head home. When you arrive, take the dogs into the yard and remove the leashes. Again, you will need one adult per dog, including the puppy. If the dogs are all right or are indifferent to the puppy, you can let your current dog inside. Then, re-leash the puppy, keeping him on the leash as you go inside.

> **FUN FACT**
> **Origins of the Pug**
>
> The Pug, half of your Puggle's genetic makeup, has a rich history dating back more than 2,000 years to the Han dynasty in China. Pugs are excellent companion dogs and were highly valued by Chinese emperors. The Chinese bred several varieties of short-nosed dogs, including the ancient Pug, which was known as the Lo-sze. Pugs are believed to have been introduced to Europe by Dutch traders in the late 16th century. The Pug even became the official dog of the House of Orange in the Netherlands after one of these loyal dogs warned William, Prince of Orange, that the Spaniards were coming in 1572. Pugs are now the 28th most popular breed in America, according to the AKC.

Put the puppy in the puppy area when the introductions are complete. Remember to make sure your current dog cannot get into this area, and your puppy cannot get out.

Introducing an Adult Dog to Other Pets

Always approach the introduction (and first few weeks together) with caution. The new adult Puggle will need his own things from the very beginning—Puggles can be territorial if not properly trained. When you aren't around, your dog should be kept in a separate area so there won't be any fighting among the dogs.

Plan for this introduction to take at least an hour. Since the dogs are both adults, they will need to move and become acquainted at their own pace.

When introducing your current dog(s) to your new dog, follow the same steps as you would with a puppy:

- Begin in neutral territory.
- Ask one adult to be present for each adult canine during the introduction.
- Introduce one dog at a time. Don't let several dogs meet your new Puggle all at once.

Bring treats to the meeting of two adult dogs—unlike with puppies. The animals will respond to the treats, and if the atmosphere becomes tense, the treats will create a distraction.

During the introduction, watch the Puggle and your dogs to see if any of them raises his hackles. This is one of the first obvious signs that a dog is uncomfortable. If the Puggle's hackles are up, back off the introductions for a little bit. Do this by calling your current dog back first. This is also when you should start waving treats around! Avoid pulling on the leashes to separate the dogs. You don't want to add physical tension to the situation because that could trigger a fight. Treats will work for all dogs, and calling their names should help get things under control.

If any of the dogs are showing their teeth or growling, call your dog back and give the dogs a chance to settle down. Use treats and a calming voice to get them to relax. You want all the dogs to feel comfortable during the first meeting, so don't force the friendship. If they seem uncomfortable or wary at first, let them move at their own pace.

Older Dogs and Your Puggle

If your current dog is older, keep in mind puppies are energetic, and they want to engage older dogs in their play. This can be very trying for your older canine, so make sure your older dog doesn't get too tired of the

Photo Courtesy of Alyssa Pucci

puppy's antics. A tired, older dog could snap and nip at your puppy in hopes of getting a little rest. You don't want your puppy to begin snapping at other dogs, too. Watch for signs your older dog is ready for some alone time, some time with you, or simply a break from the puppy.

You should always make sure your older dog has safe places where he can be alone. This is essential for those times he just doesn't feel up to being around a spry, young puppy! By keeping your puppy and your older dog separate, you can prevent the need for constant scolding. Plus, the puppy will not become wary of older dogs.

Even if you own an adult Puggle, he might be too energetic for your older dog to handle. Puggles may be active dogs at any age! Be mindful and make sure your dog's golden years are not marred by a new canine that wants to play in a way your older dog can't.

Dog Aggression and Territorial Behavior

If your Puggle is more like a Beagle, it is possible that there will be some fairly territorial behavior. With their hunting history, they can be protective of their home, growling and snarling. If your Puggle feels that someone poses a threat, he may react aggressively. It is easier to train against aggressive behavior while your dog is young. An aggressive older dog should be monitored closely and should not be left alone with other pets or children. An older Puggle has to learn how to be a part of the pack and the proper way to react to people while playing with toys and other items since Beagles can be territorial with toys too. This is why it is essential to always be firm and consistent. Your Puggle may take more after the Pug parent, but you need to make sure that you take precautions in case he has some of those Beagle tendencies.

Do not use choke chains or other negative reinforcers on your Puggle! Not only do these hurt your dog, but a Puggle does not react well to negative reinforcement because he is a very independent thinker. These types of restraints teach your dog you are not in control, and you are using a choke chain to force a certain behavior upon him. Use treats instead and/or remove the dog from any negative situation. Every time your dog does what you ask him to do, reward him. (Details on how to train your Puggle are discussed in Chapter 13.)

There are two types of aggression you should watch for:
- Dominance aggression is when your dog wants to show control over another animal or person. This kind of aggression can be seen in the

following behaviors and in reaction to anyone going near the Puggle's belongings (like toys or a food bowl):

- Growling
- Nipping
- Snapping

This is the behavior that the pack leader uses to warn others not to touch his stuff. If you see this reaction in your Puggle while he is around you, a family member, or another pet, you must intervene immediately. Correct him by saying, "No," then lavish him with praise when he stops. Remember, you must consistently intervene whenever your Puggle behaves in this manner.

Do not leave your Puggle alone with other people, dogs, or animals as long as any dominance aggression is exhibited. If you are not there to intervene, your dog will push boundaries and will likely try to show his dominance over those around him. Never train your Puggle to react aggressively!

Once you are sure this behavior has been eliminated, you can leave your current dog and Puggle alone for short periods of time. You should remain in another room or somewhere in close proximity but out of sight. Over time, you can leave your pets alone when you get the mail; then, try leaving them when you run errands or longer tasks. Eventually, you will be able to leave your Puggle alone with other dogs without worrying that he will show dominance to others.

Natural Prey Drive

Despite Beagles being fantastic hunters, Puggles are considered to have a low to average prey drive. You do need to be careful in the early days just in case your Puggle does inherit a strong prey drive, but the odds are good that you won't have much of a problem. That said, you will need to socialize your Puggle puppy with the cat long before the puppy runs free in the home. Always be present when they interact so you can correct the puppy's behavior, particularly if the puppy tries to chase the cat.

If you have other small animals, they will need to be kept in areas that your Puggle cannot access. Rabbits, rodents, ferrets, and other pets are not usually trainable. Most small animals aren't able to learn not to run away, which your puppy will likely take as an invitation to play.

Note that Beagles are particularly ardent diggers. If you have a yard, it should be enclosed by fencing. Puppies may dig out of interest, and adults may dig out of boredom. Never leave your Puggle outside alone to find out if he is more like a Pug or a Beagle.

Feeding Time Practices

Your Puggle puppy will be fed in his puppy space, so mealtime will not be a problem in the beginning.

The following are suggestions for feeding your puppy when around the other dogs; this will reduce the chance of territorial behavior:

- Feed your Puggle at the same time as the other dogs but in a different room. Keeping them separated will let your Puggle eat without distractions or feeling that your other dogs will eat what is in his bowl. Make sure to feed your Puggle in the same room each time while the other dogs eat in their established areas.
- Keep your Puggle and other dogs in their areas until they finish eating their food. Some dogs have a tendency to leave food in the bowl. Don't let them. They need to finish everything because all food bowls will be removed as soon as the dogs finish eating.
- Make sure you have someone near your Puggle so that he learns not to growl at people near his bowl. This will help reduce stress when other dogs are around the food. If your dog demonstrates any aggression, immediately correct him by saying, "No," then give him praise when he stops. Do not play with the food bowl, and make sure none of the kids play with it. Your dog needs to know that no one is going to try to steal his food.
- Over the course of a couple of weeks, move your dogs closer together while eating. For example, you can feed your current dog on one side of the door near the doorway and the Puggle on the opposite side.
- After a month or two, you can feed the dogs in the same room but with some distance between them. If your Puggle starts to exhibit protective behavior with the other dogs, correct him, then praise him when he stops the behavior.

Eventually, you can start feeding the dogs close to one another. This can take weeks to months to accomplish, depending on the age of the Puggle. A puppy will need less time because he will be socialized with the dogs from an early age, making him less wary. That does not mean he won't display territorial behavior. Yet, it likely won't take long for him to start to feel comfortable eating near the rest of the pack.

For adult dogs, this process could take longer, and you should not rush it. Let your dog learn to feel comfortable eating before you make changes, even small ones. Dogs of any breed can be protective of their food, depending on their past history. Before your dog will eat peacefully, he must be assured that his protective behavior is not necessary around other dogs. That means letting his confidence and his comfort level build at his own pace.

CHAPTER 9
The First Few Weeks

"Remember that puppies are like children and have to build their immune system. So even though everyone wants to see the new puppy, try to limit their exposure to new dogs until they have at least their second vaccine. They also need time to sleep, so during the first couple days, give them rest time throughout the day, but limit naps in the evening. This will help them be ready for bed when everyone else is too."

JENNIFER YATES
Rainbowland Puggles

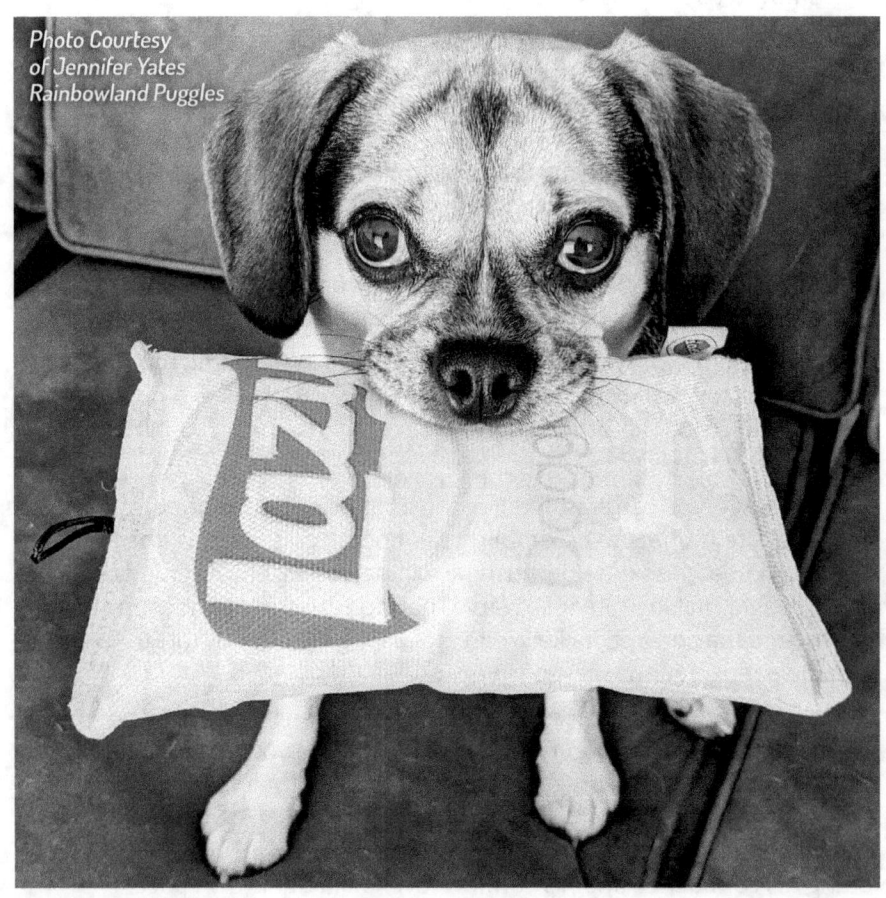

Photo Courtesy of Jennifer Yates
Rainbowland Puggles

CHAPTER 9 The First Few Weeks

The odds are good that your Puggle will want to explore his new environment the first day. When he is not sleeping, you may find yourself feeling that you can't get a moment's rest—but in a fun and entertaining way. The bond you and your Puggle form in those early days will be important in establishing the relationship you have over the years.

Your pup should be sleeping through the night after the end of that first month. If you are lucky, your dog may also have a fairly good understanding by then of where to go to the bathroom—and be willing to do it your way (though there are no guarantees since this breed is known for being difficult to housetrain). You will better understand your Puggle's personality, which will make it much easier to comfort your puppy during occasional bouts of uncertainty.

> **HELPFUL TIP**
> **Stop Jumping in Its Tracks**
>
> Because Puggles are small, especially as puppies, it might be tempting to overlook jumping as a negative behavioral trait. But it's best to stop this behavior before your dog reaches maturity. Some dog owners use the "four on the floor" technique, which encourages your dog to keep all four paws on the floor when greeting people. The basic premise of this technique is to put your dog on a leash and have another person approach and retreat from your dog. Before each approach, toss some treats on the floor in front of your dog. The other person should retreat while your dog is still finishing his treats, at first, and then extend the length of the greeting as training progresses. You will gradually decrease the number of treats given to your dog each time, until keeping all four paws on the ground becomes second nature during greetings.

The first month is when you really need to start paying attention to your puppy's emerging personality. As with all intelligent breeds, the key is to remain consistent when it comes to training. That means everyone should be consistent—including the kids. Always use what you learn about your puppy's personality to encourage good behavior!

Setting the Rules and Sticking to Them

Your puppy needs to understand the rules and to know you and your family mean them, even if the dog really doesn't like what you are saying. Once your canine learns to follow your commands, there will still be times when he will refuse to obey. That is nearly a certainty. However, he will be much more likely to listen when he knows you are in control.

Establish a No Jumping and No Mouthing Policy

If not properly trained, a Puggle may jump on you in greeting, and this can be very bad if the dog tries to jump on little children. You have the responsibility to ensure that your dog and children learn how to play properly. For your Puggle, this means no jumping on people or nipping. Any games that involve biting or nipping should always be avoided.

Nipping

There are two things that could trigger your Puggle to nip.

- One of the triggers for nipping is overstimulation. This can be one sign your puppy is too tired to keep playing or training, and you should put him to bed.
- Another trigger could be that your canine has too much energy. If this is the case, take your puppy outside to burn off some of his excess energy. At the same time, be careful not to over-exercise the puppy.

You need to be vigilant and immediately let your puppy know nipping is not acceptable. Some people recommend using a water spritzer bottle and spraying the puppy while saying, "No," after nipping. This is one of the few times when punishment may be effective. Remember—make sure your dog does not associate the spraying with anything other than his nipping.

Always firmly tell your puppy, "No," whenever he is nipping, even if it is during playtime. You should also pull away and loudly say, "Ouch!" to let your puppy know his teeth are hurting you. This will help to establish the idea that nipping is bad and is never rewarded.

Chewing

All puppies chew to relieve the pain of teething. Whether your dog is chewing on your furniture, utensils, or clothing, be sure to discourage this behavior as quickly as possible:

- Make sure you have toys for your Puggle (whether an adult or a puppy) so that you can teach him what objects are acceptable for chewing. Having a lot of available toys and rotating those toys out will give your puppy or dog several options.
- If your puppy is teething, either refrigerate a couple of toys so that they are cold or give your puppy frozen carrots. The cold will help to numb the pain. Teething usually starts at between three and four months old, and it usually ends by eight months. As discussed in Chapter 17, both parent breeds have dental issues, so you want to get toys that will be

CHAPTER 9 The First Few Weeks

Photo Courtesy of Ryan Cooper

safe for those dental issues in case your Puggle has problems. Chapter 13 also provides details on diets that may help dogs with allergies and dental problems, such as a raw diet.

- Toys that are made either of hard rubber or hard nylon are best, particularly Kongs with kibble in them. You can even fill them with water and freeze them, which will give your puppy something cool to soothe the pain of teething.

For the most part, keeping an eye on your dog when he is not in his designated space will help you quickly see when he is chewing on things he shouldn't. When this happens, firmly say, "No." If your dog continues to chew, put him back in his space. While he is in the space, make sure he has plenty of toys to chew on.

If you decide to use chew deterrents, such as bitter training sprays, be aware some dogs will not care if an item tastes bad—they will chew on it anyway. If you apply these deterrents, do not leave your dog alone and expect him to stop chewing. You should watch your dog's reaction before trusting that the bad habit is broken. Since some Puggles have separation anxiety, you should eliminate the chewing problem as quickly as possible; this will allow your pup to roam freely around your home.

Photo Courtesy of Kari Hess

Jumping

Dogs typically jump on people when they first greet them. Even though they are small, Puggles shouldn't be allowed to jump up. Use the following steps when you have a visitor (if you can, get someone who is willing to help because that will make the training that much easier):

1. Put a leash on the dog when the person knocks on the door or rings the bell. The arrival of someone will invariably excite most dogs, especially puppies.
2. Let the person in, but do not approach them until your pup calms down.
3. Be effusive in your praise when the puppy keeps all four paws on the ground.
4. If the puppy jumps on the visitor, they should turn their body and ignore him. Don't verbally correct him. Being completely ignored will be far more of a deterrent than any words you can say.
5. Give your dog something to hold in his mouth if he does not settle down. Sometimes dogs just need a task to reduce their excitement. A stuffed animal or a ball is an ideal distraction, even if your dog drops it.
6. At this point, the visitor can get low and pet your dog. Having someone on his level will make your Puggle feel he is being included. It also lets him sniff the visitor's face, which is part of a proper greeting to a dog. If your visitor is willing to help, this acknowledgment can prevent your pup from further jumping since he already feels safe with the person who is at his level.

Attention Seeking and Barking

If you are ignoring your Puggle, he may act like toddlers and young children do, resorting to any means of getting your attention even if that attention is negative. There can be different ways of acting out, like destroying something or barking. Since what he really wants is your attention, the best way to train him is by ignoring him when he acts out. If he is barking, don't acknowledge him. Once he stops barking, count to five, then praise your Puggle for the quiet. If he destroys things, remove the items so he can do no harm.

Ignoring your dog is what works best when deterring attention-seeking behavior. As difficult as that may be, it is necessary to keep your puppy from learning how to push your buttons. After all, you do not want those behaviors to escalate when he is an adult. He will be able to do a lot more damage when he is older, and his voice will be a lot louder!

If you want to train your Puggle to be a watchdog, you won't want to entirely discourage barking. You simply want to train him not to bark for attention just because he is bored.

Photo Courtesy of Stephanie Donovan

Reward-Based Training Versus Discipline-Based Training

With an intelligent breed like the Puggle, it is much more efficient to train your puppy using rewards than with punishments. This will be a particular challenge as puppies can be exuberant and are easily distracted. It is important to remember that your puppy is young, so you need to keep your temper and learn when a break from training is needed.

The following lists several critical training aspects you will need to address during the first month:

- Housetraining (Chapter 9)
- Crate training (Chapter 6)
- Barking (Chapter 11)

Find out how much house training was completed by the breeder. The best breeders may teach puppies one or two commands before the puppy goes home with you. If this is the case, keep using those same commands with your puppy so that the early training is not lost. This information can help you establish the right tone of voice to use with your puppy since he will already know what the words mean and how to react to them.

Separation Anxiety in Dogs and Puppies

Both Pugs and Beagles are considered breeds with substantial separation anxiety. Puggles are definitely known for being prone to separation anxiety, and your dog can do a lot of damage when left alone. Besides tiring out your dog before leaving home, there are other ways you can prepare your puppy or dog for long days when he is home alone.

In the beginning, keep the puppy's time alone to a minimum. The sounds of people moving around the house will help your Puggle understand the separation is not permanent. After the first week or so, alone time can involve you going out to get the mail, leaving the puppy inside by himself for just a few minutes. You can then lengthen the amount of time you are away from the puppy until he is alone for thirty minutes or so at a time.

The following are some basic guidelines for when you begin to leave your puppy alone:

- Take the puppy outside about thirty minutes before you leave.
- Tire the puppy out with exercise or playtime so that your leaving is not such a big deal.

- Place him in his puppy area—well ahead of when you plan on leaving—to avoid him associating his space with something bad.
- Don't give your puppy extra attention right before you leave. This only reinforces the idea you give attention before something bad happens.
- Avoid reprimanding your Puggle for any bad behavior that happens while you are away. Reprimanding teaches him to be more stressed because it will seem like you come home angry.

The following is a list of actions you can take to comfort your dog if you see signs of separation anxiety:

- Chew toys can give your dog something acceptable to gnaw on while you are away.
- A blanket or shirt that smells like you or other family members can help provide comfort, too. This is an ideal strategy if you have previously worn the item. (Make sure you were not in contact with any chemicals the day you wore it.) Consider giving the dog something you know you won't wear again in case he shreds it to pieces.
- Leave the puppy's area well-lit, even if it is during the day. Should something happen and you get home later than you intended, you don't want your little guy to be in the dark.
- Turn on a classical music radio station or a quiet television program—like Mr. Ed or I Love Lucy. Your goal is to prevent the house from being completely quiet so that unfamiliar noises aren't obvious.

It will not take your Puggle long to notice the behaviors that mean you will be leaving soon. Grabbing your keys, purse, or wallet will become triggers that might make your Puggle anxious. Don't make a big deal out of leaving (or returning). If you act in a normal way, over time, this will help your little one understand that your leaving is fine and that everything will be alright.

How Long Is Too Long to Be Left Home Alone?

In the beginning, your dog should spend only a brief period of time in the crate while you are gone. Though the breed is often independent, they are still pack animals. They do better when they have their pack than when they are left home alone for lengthy periods of time.

As your dog becomes housetrained and trustworthy, you should allow him to leave the crate while you are gone so that he doesn't feel he is being punished. Your new companion will not do well trapped in a crate for hours at a time!

You also need to find some good mental games that will keep your pup occupied while you are gone. Whether you bring home a puppy or an adult Puggle, it is vital that your home is "dog-proofed" before your dog's arrival. You will be glad you removed those tempting objects when your dog is crate-trained, and you leave him alone for extended periods of time.

If you are gone for several hours most days of the week, you should have a second dog to keep the Puggle company. However, nothing is quite as good as having someone home most of the day. Work to overlap your day so that your Puggle has someone to hang out with.

Don't Overdo It – Physically or Mentally

As an adult, your Puggle will probably be highly active. As a puppy, your Puggle will go from sleeping to being rambunctious to sleeping again, all within a brief period of time. A tired puppy is a lot like a tired toddler; you have to keep the little guy from becoming exhausted or from overworking those little legs. You need to be careful about harming your puppy's growing bones. Your pup is probably going to think that sleep is unnecessary, no matter how tired he is. It is up to you to read the signs that tell you when to stop all activities and to take a break or to put your pup to bed.

You should train your dog in increments of time—only for the amount of time that he can handle. Don't push your puppy's training past his concentration level, and don't discourage your adult dog by using commands that are too advanced. If you continue training your puppy past his energy levels, the lessons learned are not going to be the ones you want to teach your dog. At this age, training sessions don't need to be long; they just need to be consistent.

Walks will be much shorter during the first month. When you go outside, stay within a few blocks of home. Don't worry—by the month's end, your puppy will have more stamina, so you can enjoy longer walks with your new friend. You can also do a bit of walking on the leash in the yard if your puppy has lots of extra energy. Puppies have a tendency to attack their leash while walking because it is a distraction from running freely. Taking walks will also help your Puggle learn how to behave on the leash.

Just because your puppy can't endure long walks initially doesn't mean he won't have plenty of energy. Daily exercise will be essential, with the caveats that you need to make sure your puppy isn't doing too much, too soon and that he doesn't get too hot. Staying active will not only keep him healthy, but it will also keep him mentally stimulated. You will quickly realize how sedentary your "non-puppy life" has been because you will be on the move the entire time your puppy is awake!

CHAPTER 10
Housetraining

"To help with the house training, your puppy shouldn't be allowed to roam throughout the house until it is older and reliably potty trained. It's a great idea to have a designated area where the puppy can have free time, but make the area small at first. Then, as the puppy grows and becomes better about giving you a sign that he/she needs to go outside, you can make the space bigger."

JENNIFER YATES
Rainbowland Puggles

CHAPTER 10 Housetraining

Even with the most trainable breed, housetraining is always a chore that ranks low on the things people want to do with their puppies. This is a major element of Puggles that is nearly impossible to predict because of how different the parent breeds are. Some people claim that Puggles are quite easy to train, while others decry just how impossible it is to train their Puggles.

To improve the odds of success, plan to train your Puggle as if he is going to be difficult. With luck, you may never feel the frustration of having a dog that is difficult to housetrain.

This is where learning to be firm and consistent is really going to count. If you give your stubborn Puggle an inch, you may never be successful. Sticking to the rules will be absolutely essential. You will also need to remain calm and patient; getting upset will only reinforce undesirable behavior.

> **HELPFUL TIP**
> **Crate Training**
>
> Crate training and house-training can go hand in hand and help you reach your house-training goals more quickly and efficiently. Crates are essentially an artificial den for your dog, and they play off of your dog's instinct not to defecate where he sleeps. If you choose to use crate training as part of your housebreaking routine, be sure to choose a crate that's the appropriate size. If it's too big, your puppy will sleep in one corner and relieve itself in another. Small dogs may find it convenient to slip behind furniture to relieve themselves during the early weeks of house-training, so whenever your dog is not under direct supervision, you can place him in his crate to prevent accidents. Dogs should not spend the majority of their days crated, and puppies under six months should not be crated for more than a couple of hours at a time because they can't hold their bladders long.

Your best tool in house training a stubborn breed is to set a schedule and stick to it—no deviations!

Leashing your Puggle to go outside can help show your puppy where and when to go to the bathroom – even in your yard. However, there will still be challenges as you try to convince your puppy the designated place for the bathroom is not inside your home!

The following is a list of rules to apply when housetraining:

- Never let the puppy roam the house alone—he should always be in his dedicated puppy space when you are not watching him. No Puggle wants to spend a lot of time in a soiled crate, so being in his crate is a deterrent from doing his business there when you are not around. He may not feel the same way about other areas of your home if he is free to wander.

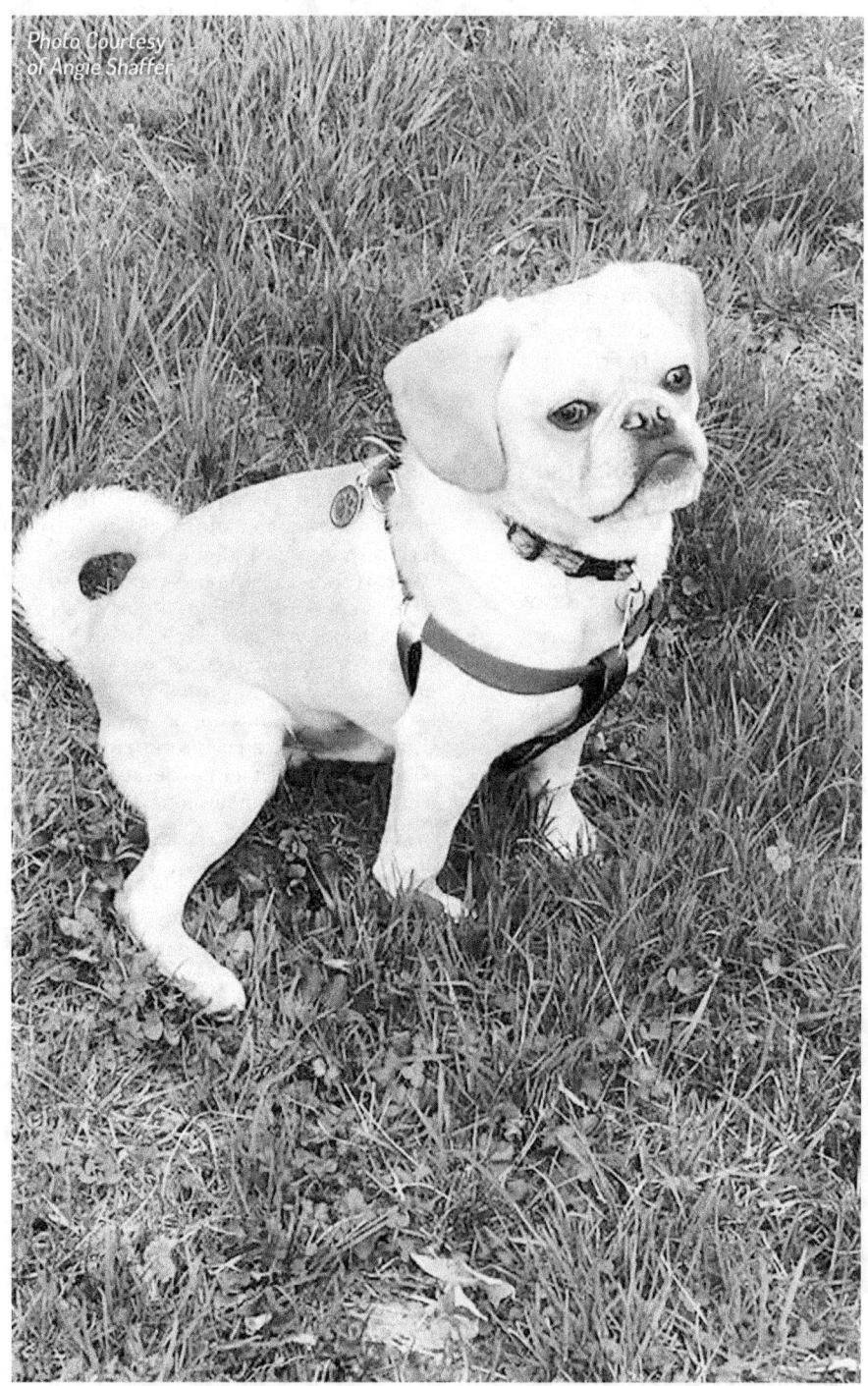
Photo Courtesy of Angie Shaffer

CHAPTER 10   Housetraining

- Give your puppy constant, easy access to the locations where you plan to housetrain him. You will need to make frequent trips outside with your puppy as he learns where to do his business. This can cause a problem if constant access to his restroom isn't always possible. When you go outside, put a leash on your puppy to make a point of where in the yard you want him to use the bathroom.

Always begin with a training plan; then, be even stricter with yourself than you are with your puppy when keeping the schedule. You are the key to your puppy's learning!

Inside or Outside – Housetraining Options and Considerations

If your breeder has already started the housetraining process, make sure to coordinate your training so that you pick up where they left off. Having someone who really knows how to housetrain a dog can give you a huge leg up on the whole endeavor—take it if you can get it!

The following is a list of housetraining options for your puppy:

- Pee pads – You should have several around the home for training, including in the puppy's area but as far from his bed as possible.
- Regular outings – Organize these outings based on your puppy's sleeping and eating schedule.
- Rewards – You can use treats in the beginning but quickly shift to praise.

Setting a Schedule

You need to keep an eye on your puppy and consistently have house training sessions:

- After eating
- After waking up from sleeping or napping
- Follow a schedule (after it has been established)

Watch for cues like sniffing and circling, which are two common signs a puppy exhibits when searching for a place to go. Start tailoring your schedule around your puppy's unique needs.

Puppies have small bladders and little control in the early days—so at this time, it isn't stubbornness but ability that is making it difficult for your puppy to follow your directions. If you train your pup to do his business inside, you need a designated space in the puppy's area for a clean pee pad. Make sure you change the pads regularly so that your puppy does not get accustomed to having waste nearby. Pee pads are better than newspapers and can absorb more. Even if you use pee pads, you should plan to transition your dog to doing his business outdoors as quickly as possible.

Photo Courtesy of Anthony DeName

CHAPTER 10 Housetraining

Choosing a Location

A designated bathroom space will make the housetraining experience easier because your Puggle will associate one area of the yard for that specific purpose. Instead of sniffing around until he finds a choice spot, have him use one spot every time, which will also make cleanup simpler, and you will be able to use the entire yard instead of having to worry about stepping in waste. Since Puggles don't do as well in cold or heat, it would be best to have a location that is fairly close to the door. That will give your dog no excuse to refuse to go to the bathroom outside. Keeping the designated area close to the door and under some kind of protection will help during inclement weather.

The perfect time to train your puppy to go to the bathroom is when you go out for walks. Between walks and using the yard, your puppy will come to see the leash as a sign that it is time to relieve his bladder, which could become a Pavlovian response.

Do not send your puppy outside alone and assume he has done what you want him to do. He needs to understand the purpose of going outside is to go to the bathroom. Until there are no more accidents in the house, you need to be sure your puppy is not losing focus. With a breed like the Puggle, it is best to always verify that your little fellow follows through. If it is hot or cold outside, and you don't make sure he takes care of business, you run the risk that he will take advantage of that lack of supervision to pretend just so he can get back inside faster. Then accidents are nearly guaranteed, even if you thought that your dog was fully trained.

Keyword Training

All training should include keywords, even housetraining. You and all family members should consistently use these keywords when housetraining your dog. If you have paired an adult with a child, the adult should be the one using the keyword during training.

To avoid confusing your puppy, be careful not to select words that you often use inside the home. Use a phrase like, "Get busy," to let your puppy know it's time to do his business. Do not use words like "bathroom" or "potty" because these words are sometimes used in casual conversation, which could trigger a desire to go to the bathroom. "Get busy" is not a phrase most people use in their daily routine, so it is not something you are likely to say unless you want your puppy to go to the bathroom outside.

Once your puppy learns to use the bathroom based on the command, make sure he finishes before offering praise or rewards.

Reward Good Behavior with Positive Reinforcement

Positive reinforcement is highly effective. In the beginning, take a few pieces of kibble with you when you are teaching your puppy where to go, both inside and outside the home. Learning you are the one in charge will help teach your Puggle to look to you for cues and instructions.

Part of being consistent with training means lavishing the little guy with praise whenever your puppy does the right thing. Use a leash to gently lead your puppy to his bathroom area with no stops in between. It will gradually become obvious to your Puggle this is where he should go to use the bathroom. Once you get outside, encourage your pup to go only when you get to the place in the yard that is intended for his bathroom spot. As soon as he does his business, give him immediate and very enthusiastic praise. Pet your puppy as you talk, and let the little guy know just how good the action was. Once the praise is done, return inside immediately. This is not playtime. You want your puppy to associate certain outings with designated potty time.

While praise is incredibly effective with Puggles, you can also give your puppy a treat after a few successful trips outside. Definitely do not make treats a habit after each trip because you do not want your Puggle to expect one every time he does his business. The lesson is to go outside, not to receive a treat every time.

The best way to housetrain in the first couple of months is to go out every hour or two, even during the night. You will need to set an alarm to wake yourself during the night so that you remember to take the puppy outside. Use the leash to keep the focus on using the bathroom, give the same enthusiastic praise, then immediately return inside and go back to bed. It is difficult, but your Puggle will get the hang of it a lot faster if there isn't a lengthy period between potty breaks. Over time, the pup will need to go outside less frequently.

Cleaning Up

Once a dog goes to the bathroom in your home, that odor will remain there for other dogs to smell, even if it's not detectable to your own nose after you've cleaned the area thoroughly. Your Puggle might take any lingering odor as a sign that the spot is an acceptable place to use the bathroom.

This means you have to be very diligent about handling accidents:

- Clean up any messes in the house as soon as you find them.

CHAPTER 10 Housetraining

- In areas where your dog has an accident, thoroughly clean the spot so that there is no remaining scent.

Spend a bit of time researching what kinds of cleaner you want to use, whether generic or holistic. For example, you will likely want to get a product with an enzyme cleaner. Enzymes help to remove stains by speeding up the chemical reaction of the cleaner with the stain. They also help to remove the smell faster, which reduces the odds your dog will continue to go to the bathroom in the same place. If your Puggle is properly trained, he will feel no need to mark his territory, but you should also discourage other dogs from claiming areas around your property.

If your Puggle has an accident, it is important to refrain from punishing the puppy. Punishment simply teaches your dog to hide his mess or to be stealthier about when he goes inside. Accidents are not a reason to punish. If they happen often, it is really more of a reflection of your training and your schedule than on the puppy. However, even the best trainers can tell you accidents are pretty much an inevitability. When it happens, tell your puppy, "No! Potty outside!" and clean up the mess immediately. Once you have finished cleaning the mess, take the puppy outside to go potty. It isn't likely that he will need to go potty again, but it is worth the attempt in case he still has a little left.

Pay attention to when these accidents happen and determine if there is a commonality between them. Perhaps you need to add an extra trip outside during the day for your puppy, or you should make a change in his walking schedule. Maybe there is something that is startling your dog and causing an accident.

CHAPTER 11
Socialization

All dogs, regardless of breed, have to learn how to interact with other canines and humans, even dogs that tend to be friendly like the Puggle. You should create time in your schedule to ensure that your dog receives socialization to bring out those fantastic personality traits that are built into his genetics. If you begin socialization when your puppy is still young, he will learn that other dogs and people can be a lot of fun. Remember that your puppy will need to have all his vaccinations before being exposed to other dogs.

Keep in mind that Puggles can be territorial. You will need to monitor behavior closely in the early days to stop any territorial behavior for things like toys. It is best to avoid having food around during socialization sessions.

Photo Courtesy of Carol Lauer

CHAPTER 11   Socialization

Another benefit of early socialization is that it can make life much more enjoyable for everyone involved, no matter what the situation. A socialized dog will approach the world from a much better place than a dog that is not socialized.

Greeting New People

Puppies will likely enjoy meeting new people, so make sure to invite friends over to help socialize your new canine family member. Your Puggle may initially react by barking, but this likely will stop as soon as the person tries to pet your pooch. Still, you will need to be careful to make sure that there are no territorial behaviors.

The following is a list of methods to use when introducing your puppy to a new person:

- Try to have your puppy meet new people daily, if possible. This could be during walks or while you are doing other activities, both in and out of the house. If you can't meet new people daily, try at least four times a week.

- Invite friends and family over and let them spend a few minutes giving the puppy their undivided attention. If your puppy has a favorite game or activity, let people know so they can play with him. This will win the little guy over very quickly and teach him new people are fun and safe to be around.

- Once your puppy is old enough to learn to do tricks (after the first month), have your little friend perform his tricks for visitors.

- Avoid crowds for the first few months. When your puppy is older, attend dog-friendly events so your pup can learn to be comfortable around a large group of people.

HELPFUL TIP
Take Them to the Store

Early and repeated socialization at a young age is one of the best ways to ensure that your dog grows up with good manners and social skills. A great way to socialize your Puggle is by taking him to pet-friendly stores. Not only will you and your dog get the opportunity to meet and greet new people and pets, but pet-friendly stores are also a great place for your dog to experience new surfaces, smells, and sounds. Because Puggles are small, you might need to keep your dog on a short leash at first, and be ready to remove yourself from any situation that feels uncomfortable or threatening. Before setting out for your local pet-friendly shop, be sure to pack treats, cleanup supplies, and a positive attitude.

Greeting New Dogs

"If you aren't 100% sure how the other dog will react – be sure to have both dogs on a leash and let them gradually check each other out. Don't ever allow your puppy to encounter a dog that is off leash or one that you don't know how they will react to your puppy. Puppies usually think that all dogs are their friends."

JENNIFER YATES
Rainbowland Puggles

Chapter 8 explained how to introduce your new Puggle to your other dogs. However, meeting dogs that are not part of your household is a little different, especially since you may encounter them at any time when you are out walking. The goal is to be able to walk around your neighborhood while your dog remains calm, refraining from running up to other dogs that may not be as friendly. The problem will likely be with the other dog, particularly if the other dog is not sociable; having a dog running toward them may be upsetting. Therefore, you need to train your Puggle as early as possible to keep him safe.

Most dogs will bow and sniff each other during an introduction. Remember to watch for signs of aggression (Chapter 8), such as raised

Photo Courtesy of Sarelle Kiel

hackles and bared teeth – it is unlikely, but it is best to be safe. Bowing, high tail, and perked ears usually mean that your Puggle is excited about meeting the other dog. If your Puggle is making noises, make sure that the sounds are playful by paying attention to the physical reaction. This applies more if you adopted an adult than if you have a puppy, but it is always a good idea to keep an eye out regardless of the age of your dog.

The best way to help a Puggle feel comfortable around unfamiliar dogs is to set up playdates with other dogs in a neutral place. This should make the whole experience much easier.

Don't let your Puggle jump up on other dogs, no matter how excited he is. This action can become a way of showing dominance, which you really don't want with your puppy, even if it is just play in the beginning. If he does jump up, immediately say, "No," to let him know it is not acceptable behavior.

The Importance of Continuing Socialization

Even friendly dogs need socialization. When family and friends visit, encourage them to bring their dogs. This will remind your Puggle his home is a welcoming place and not somewhere he needs to exert his dominance. You do not want your pup to think he can be a terror in his own house.

Socializing an Adult Dog

Socializing an adult canine requires a lot of time, dedication, gentle training, and a firm approach. There's no guarantee that your dog will be happy being around other dogs. You may be lucky enough to get an adult that is already well-socialized. That does not mean you can remain entirely relaxed! Your new dog may have had a terrible experience with a particular breed of dog that no one knows about, and this can result in a bad situation.

Your dog should be adept at the following commands before you work on socialization:

- Sit
- Down
- Heel
- Stay

"Stay" is especially important because this demonstrates your dog has self-control by remaining in one place based on your command. This quality will be helpful when socializing because using this command will allow you to control him in any aggressive situation. When you go outside, you will need to be very aware of your surroundings and be able to command your dog before another dog or person gets near.

Photo Courtesy of Melissa Bonovitz

CHAPTER 11   Socialization

- Use a short leash on walks. Being aware of your surroundings will start to cue you in regarding what is making your dog react, so you can start training your dog not to react negatively.
- Change direction if you notice your Puggle is not reacting well to a person or dog that is approaching. Avoidance is a good, short-term solution until you know your dog is more accepting of the presence of other dogs or people.
- If you are not able to take a different direction, tell your dog to sit, then block his view. This can prove to be particularly challenging as he will try to look around you. Continue to distract your dog so he will listen to you, taking his mind off what is coming toward him.
- Ask friends with friendly dogs to visit you, then meet in an enclosed space. Having one or two friendly dogs to interact with can help your Puggle realize not all dogs are dangerous or need to be put in their place. When the dogs wander around the area together, with no real interaction, your dog will learn the others are enjoying the outside, too. So, there is no reason to try to bully them!
- Get special treats for when you go walking. If your dog is aggressive when walking, have him sit and give him one of the special treats. Puggles are food motivated, so this could be a perfect way of distracting your dog from whatever is making him feel protective. At the first snarl or sign of aggression, engage the training mentality and draw upon your dog's desire for those special treats. This method is slow, but it is reliable because your dog will learn the appearance of strangers and other dogs means special treats for him. He will realize going on a walk is a positive experience, not a negative one. Nonetheless, this does not train him to interact with those dogs. Couple this tip with the previous suggestion to get the best results.

If you have ongoing problems with your adult dog, consult a behaviorist or specialized trainer.

CHAPTER 12
Training Your Puggle

Pugs and Beagles can both be incredibly difficult to train, but they can also be easy, making it that much harder to guess how trainable your Puggle will be. Most sites agree that they are not exactly an easy breed to train, so it is best to prepare for a dog that either won't pick up quickly or doesn't want to pick up training quickly.

Photo Courtesy of Sue Vidinovski

Be prepared to keep your frustration levels in check in the beginning. Whether you bring a puppy or an adult dog into the home, he has to learn the boundaries in a way that is safe and shows patience, just like with a child. If you take a few minutes to watch training videos of Puggles from the beginning, that could give you a good idea of what you could be in for when you start to train your newest family member.

Just remember—being firm, consistent, and patient will go a long way. Don't let that adorable face sway you from getting your pup to do what you instruct him to do.

> **HELPFUL TIP**
> **Small Treats for Small Dogs**
>
> There are many benefits to using positive reinforcement with your dog, including a closer relationship and a more enjoyable training experience. Because Puggles are a small breed, be sure to use an appropriately sized treat for your dog. A good rule of thumb is to make sure that the treat is smaller than a pea. Soft food that can be easily swallowed is the best option for positive reinforcement training.

Always make the early training sessions short, no matter how old your dog. Those training sessions are as much about learning how your Puggle will respond to training as it is about actually training. Puppies won't have the ability to keep focus like an adult, so a short session is ideal for keeping them from learning to ignore you. Adult dogs are going to be suspicious of you (though you may also get an adult who is already familiar with training, which could make training a little easier). And odds are, you are going to be quite tired by the end of those sessions – you'll be just as relieved as your pup to be done. As long as you are firm and consistent during those early sessions, keeping them short is in everyone's best interest.

Training will be slow going in the beginning as your dog will be quite excited for the interaction. Don't take this as an indication of your puppy's interest levels – it's more indicative of his inexperience. If you are patient with your pup from the start, you will find it will pay off later.

Benefits of Proper Training

Training is as important as socialization, and it can make general excursions easier – more importantly, training could be a way of saving your dog's life. Understanding commands might prevent your dog from running into the street, from responding to provocations from other dogs, or from acting territorially.

Training can also really benefit your relationship with your pup because it is a wonderful way to bond. This dedicated time together helps you understand your puppy's developing personality as you learn what kind of reward will work best for other tasks. Be sure your Puggle is well-trained so you can enjoy a full range of activities together—from picnics to outings in the park!

Photo Courtesy of Ryan Cooper

Choosing the Right Reward

The right reward for a Puggle will ultimately be love and affection because they adore their people. Treats are the easiest way of keying a puppy into the idea that performing tricks is good behavior, but ultimately you want your little one to follow commands without expecting food. Soon, you will need to switch to a reward that is a secondary reinforcer. Praise, additional playtime, and extra petting are all fantastic rewards for your Puggle. Your dog will probably follow you around until you decide to just sit back and relax. Plopping down to watch a movie and letting your puppy sit with you is a great reward after an intense training session. Not only did your puppy learn, but you both now get to relax together.

Because this is a smaller breed, you need to be careful about overfeeding your dog, and that includes treats. Make sure you switch to a different kind of positive reward as early as possible. Since many Puggle love their toys, you don't have to rely solely on treats as a method of praise.

If you would like your Puggle to connect positive feedback with a sound, you can use a clicker. This training tool is relatively inexpensive and should be used at the same time as you praise your puppy or dog. Clickers are not necessary, but some trainers find them useful.

Name Recognition

Over time, many of us create different names for our dogs. Nicknames, joke names, and descriptions based on some of their ridiculous actions can all be used later. However, before you can train a dog, you have to make sure he understands his real name.

The following list gives some name recognition suggestions:

1. Get some treats and show one to your dog.
2. Say the dog's name and immediately say, "Yes." (Your dog should be looking at you when you speak.) Then, give your dog a treat.
3. Wait ten seconds, then show your dog a treat and repeat step two.

Sessions shouldn't last longer than about five minutes because your dog will lose focus or interest. Name recognition is something you can do several times each day. After you have done this for five to ten sessions, the training will change a bit:

1. Wait until your dog isn't paying attention to you.
2. Call your dog. If he has a leash on, give it a gentle tug to get your dog's attention.

3. Say, "Yes," and give the dog a treat when he looks at you.

During this time, do not speak your dog's name when you correct him or for any reason other than the name recognition. This is because, in the beginning, you need to get the dog to associate his name only with something positive, like treats. This will more quickly program your dog to listen to you no matter what else is going on around him.

It is likely that your Puggle will not require a lot of time before he recognizes his name. Repetition while looking at your pup is a great way to speed up that learning process.

Photo Courtesy of Jen Jossie

CHAPTER 12   Training Your Puggle

Essential Commands

There are six basic commands that all dogs should know (Sit, Down, Stay, Come, Leave It, and Drop It). These commands are the basis for a happy and enjoyable relationship with your dog, as well as giving you a way to keep your dog safe and out of trouble. Then there are some commands that are either incredibly helpful (like Off if you don't want pets on the furniture and Quiet for a noisy dog).

Train your puppy to do the commands in the order they appear in this chapter. The last two are optional since you may allow your dog on the furniture, and he may not be a particularly vocal canine. Since dogs sit often, it is the easiest command to teach, making it the best starting point. Teaching Leave It and Drop It is much more difficult and usually requires the puppy to fight an instinct or a desire. Consider how much you give in to something you want...when you know you shouldn't! That's pretty much what your puppy is facing. Quiet can be another difficult command as dogs (particularly puppies) tend to bark in response to their surroundings. However, you don't have to teach it right from the beginning, as some puppies do grow out of it. If you finish all of the other commands and find that your dog is still a bit too noisy for your home, you can then start training, though you will need to determine just when you want them to be quiet and when you want them to bark (like when someone is outside your home). This will take some consideration on your part before you begin.

The following are some basic steps to use during training:

1. Include everyone in the home in the Puggle training. The puppy must learn to listen to everyone in the household and not just one or two people. A set training schedule may only involve a couple of people in the beginning, especially if you have children. There should always be an adult present when training, but including a child will help reinforce the idea the puppy must listen to everyone in the house. It is also an effective way for a parent to monitor a child's interaction with the puppy so that everyone plays in a way that is safe and that follows the rules.
2. To get started, select an area where you and your puppy have no other distractions, including noise. Leave your phone and other devices out of range so that you are able to keep your attention on the puppy.
3. Stay happy and excited about the training. Your puppy will pick up on your enthusiasm and will focus better because of it.
4. Be consistent and firm as you teach.
5. Bring a special treat to the first few training sessions, such as pieces of chicken or small treats.

Sit

Start to teach the command Sit when your puppy is around eight weeks old.

Once you settle into your quiet training location:

1. Hold out a treat.
2. Move the treat over your puppy's head. This will make the puppy move back.
3. Say, "Sit" as the puppy's haunches touch the floor.

Having a second person around to demonstrate this with your puppy will be helpful as they can sit to show what you mean.

Wait until your puppy starts to sit down and say, "Sit," as he sits. If your puppy finishes sitting down, give praise. Naturally, this will make your puppy excited and wiggly, so it may take a bit of time before he will want to sit again. When your puppy calms down, repeat the process.

It's going to take more than a couple of sessions for the puppy to fully connect your words with the actions. Commands are something completely new to your little companion. Once your puppy has demonstrated mastery of the command Sit, start teaching Down.

Down

Repeat the same process when teaching this command as you did for Sit:

1. Tell your dog to Sit.
2. Hold out the treat.
3. Lower the treat to the floor with your dog sniffing at it. Allow your pup to lick the treat, but if he stands up, start over.
4. Say, "Down," as the puppy's elbows touch the floor (make sure to say it as he does the action to help him associate the word with the action), then give praise while rewarding your puppy with the treat.

It will probably take a little less time to teach this command. Wait until your puppy has mastered Down before moving on to Stay.

Stay

Stay is a vital command to teach because it can keep your puppy from running across a street or from running at someone who is nervous or scared of dogs. It is important your dog has mastered Sit and Down before you teach Stay. Learning this command is going to be more difficult since it is not something your puppy does naturally.

CHAPTER 12   Training Your Puggle

Be prepared for this command to take a bit longer to teach:

1. Tell your puppy to either Sit or Stay.
2. As you do this, place your hand in front of the puppy's face.
3. Wait until the puppy stops trying to lick your hand before you begin again.
4. When the puppy settles down, take a step away. If your puppy is not moving, say, "Stay," and give a treat and some praise.

Giving your puppy the reward indicates the command is over, but you also need to indicate the command is complete. The puppy has to learn to stay until you say it is okay to leave the spot. Once you give the okay to move, do not give treats. The command Come should not be used as the okay word, as it is a command used for something else.

Repeat these steps, taking more steps further away from the puppy after a successful command.

Once your puppy understands Stay when you move away, start training him to Stay even if you are not moving. Extend the amount of time required for the puppy to stay in one spot so that he understands Stay ends with the Okay command.

When you feel that your puppy has Stay mastered, start training the puppy to Come.

Come

This is a command you can't teach until the puppy has learned the previous commands. Before you start the training session, decide if you want to use Come or Come Here. Be consistent in the words you use.

This command is important for the same reason as the previous one; if you are around people who are nervous around dogs, or if you encounter a wild animal or other distraction, this command will snap your puppy's attention back to you:

1. Leash the puppy.
2. Tell the puppy to Stay.
3. Move away from the puppy.
4. Say the command you will use for Come and give a gentle tug on the leash toward you.

Repeat these steps, building a larger distance between you and the puppy. Once the puppy seems to understand, remove the leash, and start at a close distance. If your puppy doesn't seem to understand the command, give some visual clues about what you want. For example, you can pat your leg or snap your fingers. As soon as your puppy comes running over to you, offer a reward.

Leave It

This is a difficult training command, but you need to train your dog to Leave It for when you are out on a walk and want him to ignore other people or dogs.

1. Let your dog see that you have treats in your hand, then close your hand. Your fist should be close enough for your dog to sniff the treat.
2. Say, "Leave it" when your dog starts to sniff your hand.
3. Say, "Yes," and give your dog a treat when he turns his head away from the treats. Initially, this will probably take a while as your dog will want those treats. Don't continue to say, "Leave it," as your dog should not be learning that you will give a command more than once. You want him to learn he must do what you say the first time, which is why treats are recommended in the beginning. If a minute or more passes after giving

Photo Courtesy of Kristi Prosser

CHAPTER 12   Training Your Puggle

the command, you can then issue it again, but make sure your canine is focused on you and not distracted.

These sessions should only last about five minutes. Your dog will need time to learn this command as you are teaching him to ignore something he does naturally. When he looks away and stops sniffing when you say, "Leave it," you can move on to more advanced versions of the training:

1. Leave your hand open so that your dog can see the treats.
2. Say, "Leave it" when your dog starts to show interest. This will probably be immediate since your hand will be open, so be prepared.
    a. Close your fist if your dog continues to sniff or gets near the treats in your hand.
    b. Give your dog a treat from your other hand if he stops.

Repeat these steps until your dog finally stops trying to sniff the treats. When your dog seems to have this down, move on to the most difficult version of this command.

1. Place treats on the ground or let your dog see you hide them. Then, stay close to those treats.
2. Say, "Leave it" when your dog starts to show interest in sniffing the treats.
    a. Place a hand over the treats if he doesn't listen.
    b. Give a treat if your dog does listen.

From here, you can start training while standing further from the treat with your dog leashed, so you can stop him if needed. Then, start to use other things that your dog loves, such as a favorite toy or another tempting treat that you don't usually give him.

Drop It

This is going to be one of the most difficult commands to teach because it goes against both your puppy's instincts and interests. Your puppy wants to keep whatever he has, so you are going to have to offer him something better instead. It is essential to teach the command early, as your Puggle could be very destructive in the early days. Furthermore, this command could save your pooch's life. When you are out for a walk, he will likely lunge at objects that look like food. However, once he has mastered this command, he will drop anything he picks up.

Start with a toy and a treat, or a large treat that your dog cannot eat in a matter of seconds, such as a rawhide. Make sure the treat you have is one your puppy does not get very often so that there is motivation to drop the toy or big treat.

1. Give your puppy the toy or large treat. If you want to use a clicker, too, pair it with the exciting treat you will use to help convince your puppy to drop the treat.
2. Show your puppy the exciting treat.
3. Say, "Drop it," and when he drops the treat or toy. Tell him, "Good," and hand over the exciting treat while picking up the dropped item.
4. Repeat this immediately after your puppy finishes eating the exciting treat.

You will need to keep reinforcing this command for months after it is learned because it is not a natural instinct.

Off

This is different from training your dog not to jump on people (Chapter 9). This command is specifically to get your dog off furniture or surfaces that may be dangerous. This is training you will need to do on the fly because you are training your dog to stop an action. This means you have to react to that undesirable action. Having treats on hand will be essential when you see your dog getting up on things you don't want him to be on:

1. Wait for your dog to put his paws on something you don't want him on.
2. Say, "Off," and lure him away with a treat that you keep just out of his reach.
3. Say, "Yes," and give him a treat as soon as his paws are off the surface.

Repeat this every time you see the behavior. It will likely take at least half a dozen times before your dog understands he should not perform the action anymore. Over time, switch from treats to praise or playing with a toy.

Quiet

Puggles tend to be rather quiet, but if you have a puppy that tends to bark, you may want to train the pup not to bark too often. Initially, you can use treats sparingly to reinforce quiet if your pup enjoys making noise:

1. When your puppy barks for no obvious reason, tell him to be quiet and place a treat nearby. It is almost guaranteed your dog will fall silent to sniff the treat.
2. If your dog does fall silent, say, "Good dog" or "Good quiet."

It will not take too long for your puppy to understand Quiet means no barking.

If you want your Puggle to be more of a watchdog, you will need to provide some guidance on when he should bark. He will likely bark at the door when someone is there, so it won't be as difficult to teach him to bark for

CHAPTER 12   Training Your Puggle

other reasons as well. A professional can help tailor the approach to training your dog when to bark at people at the door. Otherwise, you will want your dog to know he shouldn't be randomly barking at birds at the window or squirrels running around in the yard.

Until all of these commands are learned, it is best to avoid other types of advanced training. Between six and twelve months, you should be able to move on to tricks. Chapter 14 provides more details on tricks and games that your Puggle may love.

Where to Go from Here

If you find that training is testing your patience in all the wrong ways, you can attend different types of training classes to help you to better work with your dog to at least master the essential commands. Chapter 14 provides alternatives to helping your dog use up all of his energy, but you do need to at least ensure that your dog learns the basics. The following classes can help.

Puppy Classes

Puppies can begin to go to puppy school as early as six weeks. You will need to set aside an hour or two so that you can research schools near you. Make sure to take the time to read the reviews and see if you can talk to people who have used a particular school or trainer. Trainers should be willing to take the time to talk to you and answer questions as well, so do try talking to the people running the school. This is the beginning of obedience training, but you need to be careful around other dogs until your puppy has completed his vaccinations. Talk with your vet about when is an appropriate time to begin classes. Your vet may be able to recommend good puppy training classes in your area.

The primary purpose of these classes is socialization. Studies show one-third of all puppies have minimal exposure to unfamiliar people and dogs during the first twenty weeks of their life. This can make the outside world pretty scary! The puppy classes give you and your puppy a chance to learn how to meet and greet other people and dogs in a controlled environment. Dogs that attend these classes are much friendlier and are less stressed about such things as large trucks, thunder, loud noises, and unfamiliar visitors. They are also less likely to be nervous or suffer from separation anxiety, a likely issue for a Puggle.

Puppy classes are also great training for you! The same studies show owners who attended classes learned to react appropriately when their puppy is disobedient or misbehaves. The classes teach you how to train your puppy and how to deal with the emerging headstrong nature of your dog.

Many classes will help you with some of the basic commands, like Sit and Down. Look for a class that also focuses on socialization so that your puppy can get the most out of the instruction.

Obedience Training

After your puppy graduates from puppy school and understands most of the basic commands, you can switch to obedience classes. Some trainers offer at-home obedience training, but if you do this, it's still a good idea to also set aside regular time to socialize your pup at a dog park. If your puppy

Photo Courtesy of Jennifer Yates
Rainbowland Puggles

attends puppy classes, the trainers there can recommend classes at the next level of training. Dogs of nearly any age can attend obedience training classes, although your dog should be old enough to listen to commands before instruction begins.

Obedience training usually includes the following:
- Teaching or reinforcing basic commands, like Sit, Stay, Come, and Down.
- How to walk without pulling on the leash.
- How to properly greet people and dogs, including not jumping on them.

Obedience school is as much about training you as training your dog. It helps you learn how to train your puppy while getting your dog through basic commands and how to behave for basic tasks, like greetings and walking. Classes usually last between seven and ten weeks.

Ask your vet for recommendations, and also consider the following when evaluating trainers:
- Are they certified, particularly the CPDT-KA certification?
- How many years have they been training dogs?
- Do they have experience with training Pugs or Beagles? It is unlikely they will have experience training a Puggle.
- Can you participate in the training? If the answer is no, do not use that trainer. You have to be a part of your dog's training because the trainer won't be around for most of your dog's life.

Therefore, your dog has to learn to listen to you.

If your dog has anxiety, depression, or other serious behavioral problems, you need to hire a trainer to help your dog work through those issues. Do your research to be sure your trainer is an expert—preferably one with experience training intelligent, strong-willed dogs.

Once your Puggle understands the basic commands and has done well in obedience training, you will know if more difficult training is right for him.

CHAPTER 13
Nutrition

"Puggles really enjoy food, so weight can become an issue if their diet isn't monitored. Make sure you set times for meals and be sure you're not over feeding your dog. If your Puggle eats to quickly look into getting a 'slow feeding' bowl. These dishes will force them to eat more slowly."

JENNIFER YATES
Rainbowland Puggles

There may be many areas in which the Pug and Beagle are different, but their enthusiasm for food is nearly identical – they are gluttons. Though not generally a small dog, you will need to be very careful about how much your Puggle eats because he will be perfectly happy to perpetually eat. It is far too easy to give your dog too many treats. If everyone becomes accustomed to training the dog with praise or toys instead of treats, your dog's weight will be less problematic.

Pugs and Beagles have a number of food sensitivities, increasing the odds that your Puggle will suffer from dietary problems. A grain-free diet is recommended for breeds that tend to be more sensitive. Like other brachial breeds, Puggles tend to be prone to drooling or slobbering—it's part of the price for that cute snout. You'll get in the habit of cleaning up after your pup eats or drinks. Keeping a rag or dishcloth around the food and water bowls can make your cleanup a bit easier.

> **HELPFUL TIP**
> **Keeping an Eye on Weight**
>
> Puggles love to eat, and like any other dog, it's important to make sure that your dog maintains a healthy weight. Dogs are considered overweight when their body weight is 10-20 percent higher than their ideal body weight. It's always best to consult your veterinarian if you suspect that your dog is overweight, but there are some visual cues that you can look for at home. A good rule of thumb is that you should be able to feel all of your dog's ribs, and your dog's torso should be slightly wider than his hips. Portion control is part of a healthy plan to keep your dog feeling his best, but be sure to consult with your vet before cutting calories!

CHAPTER 13 Nutrition

Why a Healthy Diet is Important

Just because your Puggle is active doesn't mean he is burning all the calories he takes in, especially if you have an open treat policy. Just as you should not be eating all day, your puppy shouldn't be either. If you have a busy schedule, it will be too easy for your dog to have substantial lapses in activity levels while you are not ensuring the recommended daily exercise (covered in Chapter 14).

You need to be aware of roughly how many calories your dog eats a day, including treats, so be mindful of your dog's weight and if he is putting on pounds. This will tell you if you should adjust his food intake or if you should change the food to something more nutritional and with fewer calories.

Always talk with your vet if you have concerns about your Puggle's weight.

Dangerous Foods

Dogs can eat raw meat without having to worry about the kinds of problems a person would encounter. However, there are some human foods that could be fatal to your Puggle.

The following is a list of foods you should NEVER feed your dog:

- Apple seeds
- Chocolate
- Coffee
- Cooked bones (They can kill a dog when the bones splinter in the dog's mouth or stomach.)
- Corn on the cob (The cob is deadly to dogs; corn off the cob is fine.)
- Grapes/raisins
- Macadamia nuts
- Onions and chives
- Peaches, persimmons, and plums
- Tobacco (Your Puggle will not realize it is not a food and may eat it if it's left out.)
- Xylitol (a sugar substitute in candies and baked goods)
- Yeast

In addition to this list, consult the Canine Journal for a lengthy list of other dangerous foods. (http://www.caninejournal.com/foods-not-to-feed-dog/)

Photo Courtesy of Valerie Miner

CHAPTER 13   Nutrition

Canine Nutrition

Canines are largely carnivorous, and protein is a significant dietary need. However, they need more than just protein to be healthy.

The following table provides the primary nutritional requirements for dogs:

Nutrient	Sources	Puppy	Adult
Protein	Meat, eggs, soybeans, corn, wheat, peanut butter	22.0% of diet	18.0% of diet
Fats	Fish oil, flaxseed oil, canola oil, pork fat, poultry fat, safflower oil, sunflower oil, soybean oil	8.0 to 15.0% of diet	5.0 to 15.0% of diet
Calcium	Dairy, animal organ tissue, meats, legumes (typically beans)	1.0% of diet	0.6% of diet
Phosphorus	Meat and pet supplements	0.8% of diet	0.5% of diet
Sodium	Meat, eggs	0.3% of diet	0.06% of diet

The following are the remaining nutrients dogs require, all of them less than 1% of a puppy or an adult diet:

- Arginine
- Histidine
- Isoleucine
- Leucine
- Lysine
- Methionine + cystine
- Phenylalanine + tyrosine
- Threonine
- Tryptophan
- Valine
- Chloride

It is best to avoid giving your dog human foods with a lot of sodium and preservatives. Water is also absolutely essential to keep your dog healthy. There should always be water in your dog's water bowl, so make a habit of checking it several times a day so that your dog does not get dehydrated.

Proteins and Amino Acids

Since dogs are carnivores, protein is one of the most important nutrients in a healthy dog's diet. (They should not eat as much meat as their close wolf relatives do. Dogs' diets and needs have changed significantly since they have become human companions.) Proteins contain the necessary amino acids for your dog to produce glucose, which is essential for giving your dog energy. A lack of protein in your dog's diet will result in him being lethargic. His coat may start to look dull, and he is likely to lose weight. Conversely, if your dog gets too much protein, his body will store the excess protein as fat, and he will gain weight.

Meat is the best source of protein for your dog, and a dog's dietary needs are significantly different from a human's needs. If you plan to feed your dog a vegetarian diet, it is very important that you talk to your vet first. It is

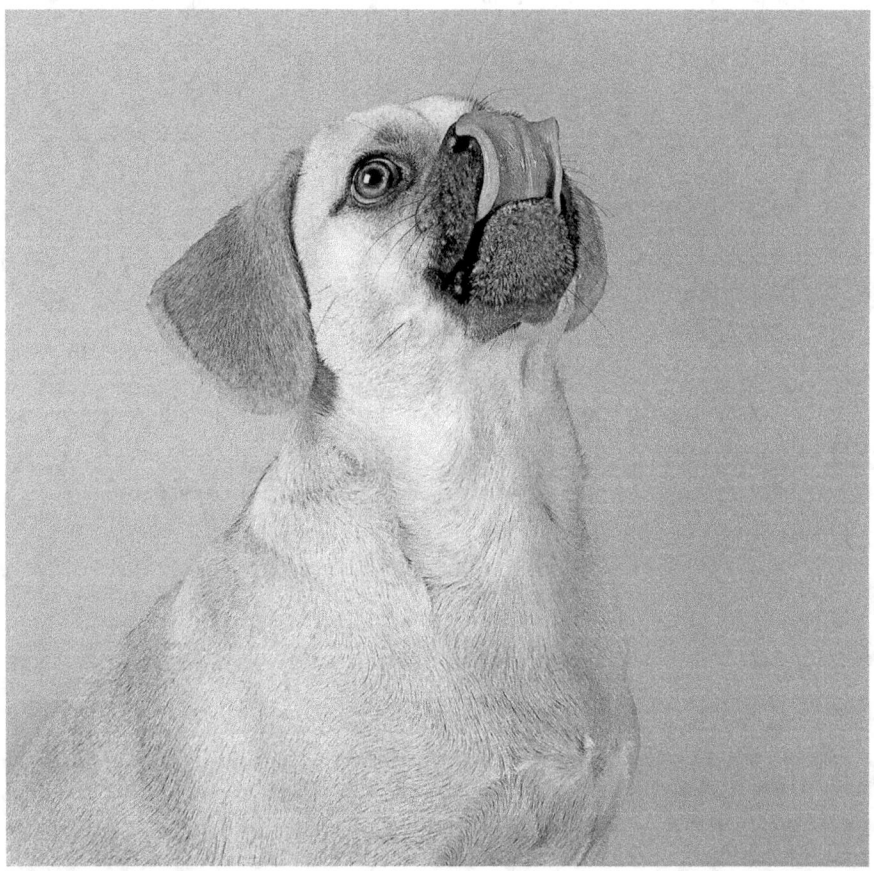

incredibly difficult to ensure that a carnivore receives adequate protein while on a vegetarian diet. Puppies in particular need to have adequate protein to be healthy adults, so you may need to give your puppy a diet with meat, then switch to a vegetarian diet after your Puggle becomes an adult.

Fat and Fatty Acids

Most fats that your dog needs are found in meat. Seed oils provide a lot of necessary healthy fats, too, with peanut butter being one of the most common sources. Fats break down into fatty acids, which your dog needs for fat-soluble vitamins that help with regular cell functions. Perhaps the most obvious benefit of fats and fatty acids can be seen in your dog's coat. Your dog's coat will look and feel much healthier when your dog is getting the right nutrients.

The following is a list of potential health issues that might arise if your dog does not get adequate fats in his daily diet:

- His coat will look less healthy.
- His skin may be dry and itchy.
- His immune system could be compromised, making it easier for your dog to get sick.
- He may have an increased risk of heart disease. The primary concern if your dog gets too much fat is that he will become obese, leading to additional health problems.

Carbohydrates and Cooked Foods

Dogs have been living with humans for millennia, so their dietary needs have evolved like our own. They can eat foods with carbohydrates to supplement the energy typically provided by proteins and fats. If you cook grains (such as barley, corn, and rice) prior to feeding them to your dog, it will be easier for him to digest those complex carbohydrates.

Different Dietary Requirements for Different Life Stages

Different stages of a dog's life have different nutritional needs:
- Puppies
- Adults
- Senior dogs

Puppy Food

During roughly the first twelve months of their lives, puppies' bodies are growing. To be healthy, they need more calories and have different nutritional needs to promote growth, so feed them a food made specifically for puppies. Puppies can have up to four meals a day. Just be careful not to overfeed them, particularly if you use treats during training. Their nutritional needs are much different than their adult counterparts.

Adult Dog Food

The primary difference between puppy food and adult dog food is puppy food is higher in calories and nutrients, which promote growth. Dog food manufacturers reduce these nutrients in adult dog food as they no longer need lots of calories to sustain growth. As a rule, when a canine reaches about 90% of his predicted adult size, you should switch to adult dog food.

The size of your Puggle is key in determining how much to feed him. The following table is a general recommendation for daily food consumption for your adult Puggle. Initially, you may want to focus on the calories as you try to find the right balance for your dog.

Dog Size	Calories
10 lbs.	420 during hot months 630 during cold months
20 lbs.	700 during hot months 1,050 during cold months

You can feed your Puggle two or three times a day, so you can divide up the calories according to this schedule. Keep in mind these recommendations are per day and not per meal. However, your Puggle will love to be eating with the family; to make sure your dog feels like a real part of the family, let your pup eat when you do, even if he doesn't get that much food at a time.

If you plan to add wet food, pay attention to the total calorie intake, and adjust how much you feed your dog between the kibble and wet food. The total calories in the kibble and wet food should balance out so as not to exceed your dog's needs. The same is true if you give your dog a lot of treats over the course of the day. You should factor treat calories into how much you feed your dog at mealtimes.

If you feed your dog homemade food, you should learn your nutrition facts, and you should pay close attention to calories instead of cup measurements.

Senior Dog Food

Senior dogs are not always capable of being as active as they were in their younger days. If you notice your dog is slowing down or suffers joint pain and shows a lack of stamina when taking long walks, you can assume your Puggle is entering his senior years. Consult with your vet if you think it is time to change the type of food you feed him.

The primary difference between adult and senior dog food is senior dog food contains less fat and more antioxidants to help fight weight gain. Senior dogs also need more protein, which will probably make your dog happy because that usually means more meat. Protein helps to maintain your dog's aging muscles. He should also be eating less phosphorus during his golden years to avoid the risk of developing hyperphosphatemia. This is a condition where dogs have excessive amounts of phosphorus in their bloodstream, and older dogs are at greater risk of developing it. The level of phosphorus in the body is controlled by the kidneys; as such, elevated levels of phosphorus are usually an indication of a problem with the kidneys.

Senior dog food has the correct number of calories for reduced activity, which means no adjustment of quantity is needed unless you notice weight gain. Consult your vet if you notice your dog is putting on weight because this could be a sign of illness.

Your Dog's Meal Options

You have three primary choices for what to feed your dog, or you can use a combination of the three, depending on your situation and your dog's specific needs:

- Commercial food
- Raw diet
- Homemade diet

Commercial Food

Make sure that you are buying the best dog food you can afford. Take the time to research each of your options, particularly the nutritional value of the food, and review this annually. Make sure the food you are giving your dog is high quality, and always take into account your dog's size, energy levels, and age. Your puppy may not need puppy food for as long as other breeds, and dog food for seniors may not be necessary for Puggles. You'll need to pay attention to your dog's individual needs to determine if they need a special food for their age.

The website Pawster provides several great articles about which commercial dog foods are best for Puggles. Since new foods frequently come on the market, check periodically to see if there are new, better foods that have become available.

If you aren't sure which brand of food is best, talk with the breeder about the foods they recommend. Breeders are really the best guides for you here, as they are experts, but you can also ask your vet.

Some dogs may be picky eaters who get tired of repeatedly eating the same food. While you shouldn't frequently change the brand of food because that can upset your dog's stomach, you can get foods that have assorted flavors. You can also change the taste by adding a bit of wet (canned) food. Adding one-fourth to one-third of a can for each meal is an easy change to make to ensure your dog's happiness.

For more details on commercial options, check out the website Dog Food Advisor. They provide reviews on various dog food brands as well as providing information on recalls and contamination issues.

Commercial Dry Food

Dry dog food often comes in bags, and it is what the vast majority of people feed their dogs.

Dry Dog Food

PROS	CONS
• Convenience	• Requires research to ensure you don't buy doggie junk food
• Variety	• Packaging is not always honest
• Availability	• Recalls for food contamination
• Affordability	• Loose FDA nutritional regulations
• Manufacturers follow nutritional recommendations (not all of them follow this, so do your brand research before you buy)	• Low quality food may have questionable ingredients
• Specially formulated for different canine life stages	
• Can be used for training	
• Easy to store	

CHAPTER 13   Nutrition

The convenience and ease on your budget mean you are almost certainly going to buy kibble for your dog. This is perfectly fine, and most dogs will be more than happy to eat kibble. Be sure you know what brand you are feeding your dog, and pay attention to kibble recalls so you can stop feeding your dog if necessary. Check out the following sites regularly for recall information:

- Dog Food Recalls – www.dogfoodadvisor.com
- American Kennel Club – www.AKC.org (Even if the Puggle isn't recognized by the organization, dog food recalls are for every breed that eats a particular food.)
- Dog Food Guide – www.dogfood.guide

Commercial Wet Food

Most dogs prefer wet dog food over kibble, but it is also more expensive. Wet dog food can be purchased in large packs that can be extremely easy to store.

Wet Dog Food

PROS	CONS
• Helps keep dogs hydrated • Has a richer scent and flavor • Easier to eat for dogs with dental problems (particularly those missing teeth) or if a dog has been ill • Convenient and easy to serve • Unopened, it can last between 1 and 3 years • Balanced based on current pet nutrition recommendations	• Dog bowls must be washed after every meal • Can soften bowel movements • Can be messier than kibble • Once opened, it has a very short shelf life, and should be covered and refrigerated • More expensive than dry dog food, and comes in small quantities • Packaging is not always honest • Recalls for food contamination • Loose FDA regulations

Like dry dog food, wet dog food is convenient, and picky dogs are much more likely to eat it than kibble. If your dog gets sick, use wet dog food to ensure that he is still eating and gets the necessary nutrition each day. It may be harder to switch back to kibble once your Puggle is healthy, but you can always add a little wet food to make each meal more appetizing.

Raw Diet
- For dogs prone to food allergies (the Puggle is too new to know if the breed is prone to this problem, so it is best to monitor your dog and his diet from the early days), raw diets can help prevent an allergic reaction to wheat and processed foods. Raw diets are heavy in raw meats, bones, vegetables, and specific supplements. Some of the benefits of a raw diet include:
- Improves your dog's coat and skin
- Improves immune system
- Improves health (as a result of better digestion)
- Increases energy
- Increases muscle mass

Raw diets are meant to give your dog the kind of food dogs ate before being domesticated. It means giving your dog uncooked meats, whole (uncooked) bones, and a bit of dairy products. It doesn't include any processed food of any kind—not even food cooked in your kitchen.

However, there are potential risks to this diet. Dogs have been domesticated for millennia, and their digestive systems have also evolved. Trying to force them to eat the kind of diet they ate hundreds of years ago does not always work as intended, primarily because they may not be able to fully digest raw food the way their ancestors did.

There are also many risks associated with feeding dogs uncooked meals, particularly if the food has been contaminated. Things like bacteria pose a serious risk and can be transferred to you if your dog gets sick. Many medical professionals also warn about the dangers of giving dogs bones even if they are uncooked. Bones can splinter in your dog's mouth and puncture the esophagus or stomach.

The Canine Journal—www.caninejournal.com—provides a lot of information about a raw diet, including different recipes and how to transition your dog to this diet. Always talk to your veterinarian before putting your dog on a new kind of diet.

Homemade Diet

The best home-cooked meals should be planned in advance so that your Puggle gets the correct nutritional balance. Typically, 50 percent of your dog's food should be animal protein (fish, poultry, and organ meats). About 25 percent should be full of complex carbohydrates. The remaining 25 percent should be from fruits and vegetables, particularly foods like pumpkin, apples, bananas, and green beans. These foods provide extra flavor your Puggle will probably love while filling him up faster and reducing the chance of overeating.

The following are a few sites where you can learn how to make homemade meals for canines. Some of them are not breed-specific, so if you have more than one dog, these meals can be made for all your furry, canine friends:

- Homemade Dog Food with a Special Ingredient
- Homemade Food for Pugs
- Easy Healthy Homemade Dog Food (and the Sweet Pug That Inspired It)
- Loves Pugs
- Beagles Life
- Beagle Pro
- DIY Homemade Dog Food
- DORG Daily Diet
- Dogsaholic

Keep in mind the foods your Puggle absolutely should not eat. You can also mix some of the food you make for yourself into your Puggle's meal. Do not feed your Puggle from your plate! Split the food, placing your dog's meal into a bowl so that your canine understands your food is just for you.

Scheduling Meals

Your Puggle will likely expect you to stick to a schedule, which definitely includes mealtimes. If treats and snacks are something you establish as a normal routine, your dog will expect that, too!

For puppies, plan to have three or four meals, while adults and seniors should typically have two meals a day.

Food Allergies and Intolerance

Whenever you start your dog on a new type of food (even if it's simply a different flavor), you need to monitor him while he becomes accustomed to the change. Food allergies are fairly common in Puggles, and the symptoms

Photo Courtesy of Angie Shaffer

manifest themselves as hot spots, which are similar to rashes in humans. Your dog may start scratching or chewing specific spots on his body, and his fur could start falling out around those spots.

Some dogs don't have individual hot spots, but the allergy shows up on their entire coat. If your Puggle seems to be shedding more fur than normal, take him to the vet to be checked for food allergies.

If you give your dog something his stomach cannot handle, it will probably be obvious when your dog is unable to hold his bowels. If he is already housetrained, he will probably either pant at you or whimper to let you know he needs to go outside. Get him outside as quickly as you can so that he does not have an accident. Flatulence will also probably occur more often if your Puggle has a food intolerance.

Since the symptoms of food allergies and intolerances look similar to a reaction to nutritional deficiencies, you should visit your vet immediately! This is especially true if you notice any problems with your dog's coat or skin.

CHAPTER 14
Playtime and Exercise

With parents that have very different energy levels, guessing your Puggle's energy levels will be like trying to predict the weather next week. Fortunately, they aren't a large breed, so even if your canine is more energetic, working off that energy won't be too much trouble. In fact, 30-minute sessions twice a day will be just as good for you to get out and walk as they are for your Puggle. There are several important benefits to ensuring your dog gets adequate activity – both for you and your pup:

- It helps keep your dog at a healthier weight.
- He is tired enough not to be too much trouble, especially if you need to leave him alone for a little while. A more intelligent dog will entertain himself, so getting your little friend tired first could help reduce destructive behavior.
- It is a great time to bond.

Photo Courtesy of Bethany Whitaker

CHAPTER 14 Playtime and Exercise

Exercise Needs

If your Puggle is more like the Pug parent, 30 minutes will be enough to keep your pup happily tired. If he takes after the Beagle, though, plan for at least an hour a day – though you can break it up into a couple of sessions every day. It's much easier to get an hour of exercise every day when you break it into two or more exercise sessions. This will be vital during the hotter months because brachial dogs shouldn't be out in the heat for long. Walk in the early morning and once or twice in the evening.

Rainy and cold days may prove to be a bit trickier as you may not be too happy with being outside. Your dog may or may not mind. If either (or both) you or your dog aren't too interested in going out in inclement weather, there are plenty of other ways to get exercise inside.

In addition to physical exercise, it is important to ensure your dog gets enough mental stimulation. Planning for a walk or play session before leaving home ensures that potentially destructive and nervous tendencies will be minimized.

> **HELPFUL TIP**
> **Choosing the Right Hike**
>
> Puggles are a small breed, and they may not be the first dog that comes to mind when you think "hiking buddy," but with some preparation and foresight, you and your Puggle can enjoy hitting the trails in the great outdoors. When choosing a hike suitable for a small-breed dog, first check the trail's rules to make sure that dogs are permitted. Then you'll want to make sure you start small and choose a hiking trail that has an "easy" rating on one of the trail-rating apps such as AllTrails. Be sure to pack plenty of snacks and water for you and your dog, and come up with a plan for transporting your dog back to the car if he gets overly tired. Keep an eye out for signs of exhaustion or overheating, and don't forget to talk to your vet before starting any new or strenuous exercise with your Puggle.

Outdoor Activities

Even if your dog doesn't end up being a particular fan of outdoor activities, there are some things that your pooch will almost certainly enjoy doing.

Chase

All you have to do to initiate this game is start running away from your Puggle. The faster you move, the faster your dog will go to stay as close to you as possible. It really won't take very long to get your dog tired enough to go lounge somewhere.

This is a game where you can definitely involve the whole family. If you have kids, you can take the dog and kids out and have them play around in the yard, then break out the sprinkler or kiddie pool to cool them down.

If you want to do the pursuing, it's as easy as turning around, throwing your arms in the air, and making a loud noise. Your Puggle will probably figure out really quickly that he's supposed to turn and run from you. This game often ends with you flopping on the ground and letting your pup lick your face as you laugh. It's quite an entertaining game with such an adorable dog.

Tricks – for Fun!

Your dog may not be keen on training, but then again, he may be thrilled with the idea. If your Puggle enjoys training, tricks are something that your dog may enjoy. It's a fantastic way to bond and to tire your dog out with minimal exertion on your part. The best way to get ideas for this is to go online and look for videos of tricks you can teach Puggles, Pugs, and Beagles. You will need to finish all of the commands from Chapter 12 before you try teaching your dog to do tricks, but once your dog does know and reliably respond to those commands, you can start teaching him to do things like roll over, dance, and play dead.

Photo Courtesy of Julianna Montez

CHAPTER 14 Playtime and Exercise

Photo Courtesy of Carole Robinson

Great Walking Companion

As long as it isn't too hot or too cold outside, a nice 20- to 30-minute walk around the neighborhood two or three times a day is the perfect daily exercise for you and your dog. Your Puggle will likely be bouncy and proud or curious and excited as you stroll around the blocks. If there is a nearby park, this will be a great place to go. It isn't likely that your dog will need a frequent change of venue for the walks, making it easier to walk with your pup on a regular basis.

Water Activities

Some Puggles enjoy playing in water. From sprinklers to kiddie pools, there are plenty of different activities you can do with your pooch. A kiddie pool provides the perfect way to cool down your dog and to tire the pooch out with minimal effort on your part. Easy to set up on a hot day, it can also help strengthen your dog's muscles. Swimming in a kiddie pool is fantastic for keeping your Puggle's joints healthy.

Dog Parks

Since there are fantastic odds that your Puggle is going to be sociable, taking time a couple of days a week to head to a dog park will mean other dogs can tire your pupper out. Give him about 30 minutes of playtime, and he'll probably be more than ready to go home. During the summer, plan to go in the early to middle of the morning. It's a great way to socialize your dog, though you will need to be careful in the early days to make sure your dog enjoys the playtime. If your dog doesn't seem particularly happy being with other dogs, this may not be the best way to spend time outside the home.

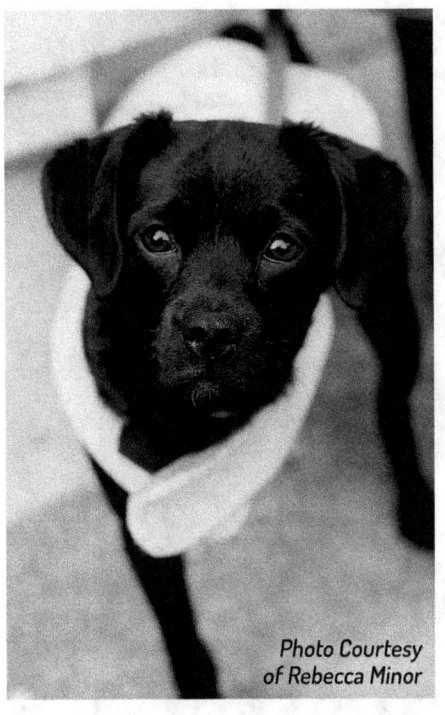

Photo Courtesy of Rebecca Minor

Indoor Activities

If your Puggle is a homebody, you'll definitely want options to entertain him. You'll also need plenty of options for rainy, hot, and colder weather. Fortunately, there are many indoor games that will be just as effective as any outdoor activity.

Hide and Seek

Hide and seek is a game you can play once your dog understands proper behavior in the home. Since your Puggle will probably hear you wherever you hide, you can also make it a game of hide the toy. If you distract your pup while someone else hides the toy, your Puggle will have a fun time trying to locate it!

Pillow and Blanket Forts

Building a pillow or blanket fort in your home will be a great way to keep your kids and your dog active. They can play hide and seek in the fort, crawl around, and generally treat it like their own little castle. Your dog will be very excited about bounding around in the fort, giving you a lot of opportunities to take some adorable pictures.

Ice Cube Escape!

If your Puggle takes an interest in this game, it can help to cool him down while giving him a way to play without you having to be engaged for most of the playtime. Simply put an ice cube on vinyl (it won't work on carpet or tile), and let your dog try to pick it up. If you have the right-sized cube, this will be a particularly difficult task, resulting in the dog looking silly as the ice slides away from him. Smaller square cubes are best. Half-crescent ice cubes tend to be easier to pick up, so they may not work so well with your Puggle.

This could result in a bit of clean-up, especially if your Puggle simply gives up and lets the ice cube melt on the floor. Even if your dog manages to catch and eat the ice, there are good odds there will be water on the floor, as well as a bit of slobber. A small price to pay for the pleasure of seeing your Puggle having such a great time.

Laser Pointers

They aren't just for cats. If you don't want to use a toy for chase, try getting your Puggle to chase a laser pointer. This may or may not work as your Puggle may realize that he can't catch it—but if that desire to hunt kicks in, it'll probably be a game you can play for quite some time before your pup wants to do something else. It is a terrific way to expend energy on rainy or chilly days! Being excited yourself can really sell this for your pup to join in the fun.

Puzzle Toys!

Puzzle toys are a fun way to get your dog to move around without you having to do much. Most puzzle toys are food-based, so the dog will need to figure out how to get the treats out. If you use these toys, keep in mind that your dog isn't likely to work off the extra calories consumed from puzzle treats.

What to Avoid

There are a lot of things you can do to exercise a Puggle, but there are also several things to avoid besides jogging.

Activities That Could Hurt Their Backs

Pugs can have problems with their spines, with a small percentage having spinal deformities. Your Puggle isn't as likely to have this problem, but you will still want to make sure you are always careful not to do anything that may put unnecessary stress on your dog's back. This is especially true if your Puggle has the curly Pug tail.

Chapter 17 provides more details about potential back issues, but there are things that you can do that could make the problem worse. Never picking up your dog is definitely important. Chasing balls or other toys and jumping can hurt him, especially if he doesn't land right. Be careful when playing any games where your dog may fall or run into something.

Leaving Them Alone Outside

Because your Puggle is a medium-sized dog, you don't have to worry about him being snatched by a bird of prey, but that doesn't mean he is safe. Beagles have been chasing and digging for centuries, and your fence isn't going to stop your little friend. When it's time to go out to the bathroom, always go with your dog to make sure he isn't making a break for it.

Yes, putting your dog out in the backyard alone is easier, especially if you are running late for work or it's snowing or raining. But the time you save is negated if your dog manages to get out of your yard because you weren't watching him. Never put your dog outside and hope that he will get his daily exercise. It's an activity that requires both of you – especially since your bored Puggle will learn that getting out of the yard will get him more attention as you try to chase him.

Off Leash

Neither of the parent breeds is known for being obedient, and Beagles are known for getting tunnel vision when they smell a new scent. Trying to get the attention of a Beagle on a scent trail is next to impossible. Because of this, unless you are at a dog park or in a fenced-in location, don't take your Puggle off the leash.

Even if your dog does seem to listen to you during training, Beagles have centuries of being followed by their humans. Trying to call out to your Puggle to get him to stop is not likely to be effective when he is running away

CHAPTER 14 Playtime and Exercise

because he will expect you to chase behind him – that's how a Puggle's breeding works. He takes off, and his people follow him. Avoid something that is dangerous to both you and your Puggle, and just keep him on the leash.

Photo Courtesy of Vinny Parrish

CHAPTER 15
Grooming – Productive Bonding

Puggles are shedders, but really not any worse than any other short-coated dog. Tending to their coats will actually be fairly easy, and grooming this breed is best described as moderate grooming (largely to keep the shedding to a minimum).

In addition, there are other regular grooming tasks you will need to do, including taking care of your Puggle's teeth and toenails.

Grooming Tools

Puggle's have a double coat, which means they have a lot of fur, even if it does tend to be shorter in length. Some Puggles can have fur that is considered medium in length, which means the fur rolling in little balls around your home will be more noticeable. The Puggle undercoat is dense and short, keeping them warm during the cooler months. The top-coat is longer and is typically easy to manage.

You don't need a lot of tools to properly groom your Puggle. However, make sure you have the following items on hand:

- A pin brush or bristle brush (Bark Space provides some details on the different types of brushes.)
- Curry brushes and combs aren't necessary, but they can be incredibly useful when your dog decides to play in the mud or gets mats after romping in the woods or fields.
- A shedding tool can help during the times when your Puggle is shedding more than usual. Shedding tools help to remove the extra fur from both coats, not just the top coat.

> **HELPFUL TIP**
> **Choosing the Right Brush**
>
> Pugs and Beagles are both considered heavy-shedding breeds, due in part to their double coats. Routine brushing will help eliminate the amount of fur shed in your home and on your clothes, but which brush will do the best job? A pin brush used in combination with a bristle brush is a great basic combo for tackling the two layers of your Puggle's coat. Both of these brushes are gentle on your dog's skin and will remove loose hair and dirt from his coat.

CHAPTER 15 Grooming – Productive Bonding

Photo Courtesy of Nola Klaubert

- Shampoo (Make sure you use dog shampoo, not human, and check Bark Space for the latest recommendations.)
- Nail trimmers
- Toothbrush and dog toothpaste (not human—it's toxic!). (Check the American Kennel Club for the latest recommendations for the parent breeds, particularly the Pug, as they tend to have dental problems.)

Photo Courtesy of Julianna Montez

Coat Management

Despite being a designer breed, coat management is actually fairly easy to predict with Puggles (something that is not true of most other designer dogs). In terms of brushing, plan to brush at least once a week. This will keep the fur from matting while also reducing how much fur you have floating around your home.

A good rule of thumb is once a week, but there are definitely times when you will need to brush more frequently, like if you have a puppy and when your dog gets older. Every breed has different grooming needs at different stages of life.

Puppies

The difficulty when grooming a puppy is fairly universal because puppies are notorious for squirming! A daily brushing is the best way to both reduce how much your puppy sheds and to bond with your dog. Yes, it will be a bit challenging in the beginning because puppies don't sit still for prolonged periods of time; there will be a lot of wiggling and attempts to play. Trying to tell your puppy that the brush is not a toy clearly won't work, so be patient during each brushing session!

On the other hand, your pup will be so adorable that you probably won't mind a grooming session taking a bit longer than expected. Just make sure you let your pup know grooming is serious business, and playing comes after grooming. Otherwise, your Puggle is going to always try to play, which will make brushing him more time-consuming.

Try planning to brush your puppy after a vigorous exercise session so that your Puggle has far less energy. If you find your puppy has trouble sitting still, you can make brushing sessions shorter but do it more than once a day until he gets used to the routine.

Adult Dogs

Brushing your dog at least once a week is adequate to get rid of dead skin cells and loose fur. Grooming mitts can make this task faster because it allows you to brush a large section of the coat with each stroke. Whether you use a glove or a brush, the weekly brushing is both relaxing to your pup and beneficial for his skin. The grooming process stimulates the skin to release oils that make the fur shinier and more resistant to dirt. Yes – if you regularly brush your dog, it can help reduce how much you have to bathe your Puggle.

Brushing your dog is about more than just removing excess fur and improving the coat's shine. You need to spend each grooming session looking for skin problems, lumps, flea or tick bites, and other problems when you brush your buddy. This will indicate a potential problem, which you should keep an eye on with a trip to the vet if symptoms are severe. You will also need to carefully clean out the wrinkles that your dog has, especially around the face. A damp cloth (make sure it isn't wet, just damp) can be quickly run through and around the wrinkles to remove any dirt that has gotten into the folds.

Photo Courtesy of Debbie Ying

CHAPTER 15   Grooming – Productive Bonding

If you rescued an adult Puggle, it might take a little while to get the dog used to being brushed frequently. If your dog does not feel comfortable in the beginning when you brush his fur, work the routine into your schedule, just like training, so he will get accustomed to the task.

Senior Dogs

You can brush your senior dog more often if you would like, as the extra affection and time you give him will likely be welcome. After all, he's slowing down, and just relaxing with you will be enjoyable for him (and the warmth of your hands will feel really good on his aging body). Grooming sessions are an appropriate time to check for problems while giving your older pup a nice massage to ease any pain. Look for any changes to the skin, such as bumps or fatty lumps. These may need to be mentioned to the vet during a regular visit.

Allergies

Some Puggles have skin allergies because this is a problem with both parent breeds. If your Puggle is suffering from hot spots, or if you notice his coat is thinning, then you should look for the following allergic reactions:

- Wounds take longer to heal
- Weak immune system
- Aching joints
- Hair is falling out
- Ear infections

Regular brushing keeps you aware of the health of your Puggle's coat. This will help you identify when your little dear is suffering from allergies so you can take him to the vet immediately.

Bath Time

Since regular brushing helps stimulate the natural oils of the breed, most Puggle people recommend just bathing as needed. If you prefer to be able to set a schedule, once a quarter (once every three months) or twice a year will probably keep your Puggle from getting stinky. If your Puggle gets muddy or really dirty, make sure to bathe him so that the dirt and mud don't get trapped in the wrinkles. Avoid bathing him too often since it can irritate your dog's skin and remove necessary oils in his fur.

9 STEPS FOR BATH TIME

1. GET EVERYTHING YOU WILL NEED IN ONE PLACE
Make sure you have the following supplies ready: shampoo and conditioner (made for dogs), one large cup, towels, brush, non-slip tub mat.

2. TAKE YOUR PUGGLE OUT FOR A WALK.
This will both tire your dog and make him a little hotter, which will make the bath less hated – maybe even appreciated.

3. RUN THE WATER
Make sure that the temperature is lukewarm but not hot, especially if you have just finished a walk. If you are washing him in a bathtub, you only need enough water to cover up to your pup's stomach.

4. TALK IN A STRONG CONFIDENT VOICE
Don't use baby talk. Your Puggle needs a confident leader, not to be treated like an infant.

5. PLACE THE DOG IN THE TUB
and use the cup to wash the dog. Don't use too much soap – it isn't necessary. You can fully soak the dog starting at the neck and going to the rump. It is fine to get him wet all at once, then to suds him up, or you can do it a bit at a time if your dog is very wiggly. Just make sure that you don't get any water on his head.

6. TALK TO YOUR DOG
while you are bathing him, keeping in mind you need to talk with confidence, not a high tone.

7. MAKE SURE YOU DON'T GET WATER IN YOUR DOG'S EYES OR EARS
You don't need to get water on the top of your dog's head. Use a wet hand and gently scrub around his eyes and ears, being careful to avoid getting soap or water in either.

8. RINSE OFF AGAINST THE GRAIN
Make sure to rinse the water up against the natural lay of the fur so that there isn't any shampoo left beneath the hairs.

9. TOWEL DRY AND BRUSH
Towel drying and brushing are great bonding times, towel dry and then brush gently so your Puggle enjoys the process and is excited for the next bath!

CHAPTER 15 Grooming – Productive Bonding

Whenever you go exploring or hiking with your Puggle, most likely, you will need to bathe your canine after each adventure. Make sure the water isn't too cold or too hot but comfortably warm, and always avoid getting his head wet. Washing your dog's face is covered in the next section.

You can use these practices with other kinds of bathing, such as outside or at a public washing facility; modify them, as necessary.

The first few times you bathe your dog, pay attention to the things that bother or scare your Puggle. If he is afraid of running water, make sure you don't have the water running when your dog is in the tub. If he moves around a lot when you start to apply the shampoo, it could indicate the smell is too strong. Modify the process as necessary in order to make it as comfortable for your dog as possible.

Keep a calm, loving tone as you wash your dog to make the process a little easier next time. Sure, your Puggle may whine, throw a tantrum, or wiggle excessively, but a calm reaction will teach your dog that bathing is a necessary part of being a member of the pack.

Cleaning Eyes and Ears

When bathing your dog, use a washcloth to wash his face and ears, and ALWAYS avoid getting water in his ears, which can lead to problems.

You will need to make weekly checks around your Puggle's eyes and ears to detect infections early, especially if your dog has wrinkles. The following are signs of a problem:

- Frequent head shaking or tilting
- Regular scratching at ears
- Swollen or red ears
- A smell or discharge from the ears

If you notice any problems with your Puggle's ears, make an appointment with your vet. Never try to treat an infection on your own; hydrogen peroxide, cotton swabs, and other cleaning tools should never be used in a dog's ears. Your vet can show you how to clean your dog's ears correctly.

Puggles have a few genetic eye and ear conditions (See Chapter 17), so take time to always check your dog's eyes while you are grooming him.

Cataracts are a fairly common problem for all dogs as they age. If you see cloudy eyes, have your Puggle checked.

Trimming Nails

Cutting a Puggle's nails can be difficult because dogs can be sensitive about someone touching their paws. Odds are your dog will have dark nails, which makes it difficult to cut them to the correct length without accidentally cutting the quick, the most sensitive part of the nail. It's best to have an expert cut your dog's nails until you understand how nail trimming is done. If you have never cut a dog's nails, ask a professional, like a groomer or a vet, to teach you the steps involved because nails can bleed a lot if they are not cut properly. If you know how to trim a dog's nails, make sure to have some styptic powder nearby in case you cut the nail too close.

If you want to trim your dog's nails yourself, there are nail grinders that can help lessen your worry about cutting the quick, but you will need to make sure you don't grind too much off the nail. Seek help from a professional before using the grinder, keep your dog calm during the process, and always think of your dog's safety first.

To know when your pup needs his nails cut, listen for clicking sounds on the hard surfaces when your dog is walking. Those clicking sounds indicate you should trim your dog's nails on a more frequent basis. As a general rule, once a month is recommended.

If you decide to trim your dog's nails, you should always watch a professional do it first. If you then want to do it yourself, you will need to be very careful and keep an eye out to make sure that you don't cause your dog's nail to bleed. It would probably be best to have a professional watch you first as dogs' nails can bleed a lot if you cut them too much.

Dogs' nails have a small vein that runs through them, and for dogs with white nails, you can see the pink vein. If your dog has black nails, never try to cut his nails without getting professional assistance a few times because you cannot see where that vein ends, and you will need to learn to avoid cutting the nail too much.

Once you are comfortable cutting your dog's nails, you will need a set of nail clippers for small to medium-sized dog paws (depending on the size of your Puggle).

1. Take your dog's paw gently and firmly. If your dog squirms, you may need to tire out your dog before trying to cut his nails.
2. Push any hair away from the nail you want to cut.
3. Look for the pink vein (if your dog has light-colored nails), then be mindful of it as you prepare to cut the first nail.
4. Position the nail clipper where the nail begins to curve, making sure the vein is not going to be cut.

CHAPTER 15   Grooming – Productive Bonding

5. Check the under part of the nail to see if you can see a pinkish-grey area. If you can see it, do not cut any further. If you don't see it and you want to cut a little more, repeat step four.

* If your dog's nail starts to bleed, apply styptic powder or silver nitrate sticks (the sticks are less messy) to the area. Follow the directions on the container to help stem the flow. Continue to hold your dog's paw until it stops bleeding before you let go of your dog. You can use hydrogen peroxide to clean up the blood on the fur after the nail stops bleeding.

You will need to repeat this process for every nail on all four paws.

If you only cut a little each time, you will need to cut your dog's nails once a month. If you cut a little further, you may be able to cut his nails once a quarter.

Oral Health

Since Puggles tend to have dental issues, it is best to be careful with your Puggle's dental care. This means being vigilant about oral hygiene. Your dog will benefit from the extra care you give his teeth.

Besides healthy food, there are two recommendations to take care of your Puggle's teeth.

1. Brush your Puggle's teeth twice a week.
2. Give your Puggle dental chew treats.

Brushing Your Dog's Teeth

You have to learn to be patient and keep teeth cleaning from being an all-out fight with your dog. Brushing a dog's teeth is a little weird, and your Puggle may not be terribly happy with someone putting stuff in his mouth. However, once he is accustomed to it, the task will likely only take a few minutes a day. Regular brushing keeps down plaque and tartar, making your pup's teeth healthier.

Always use a toothpaste that is made for dogs; human toothpaste can be toxic for your little friend. There are assorted flavors of dog toothpaste, which will make it easier when brushing your Puggle's teeth, and it could also be entertaining as he tries to eat the meat-flavored toothpaste!

Once your dog seems comfortable with having his teeth brushed with your finger, try the same steps with a canine toothbrush. (It could take a couple of weeks before you can graduate to this stage.)

Dental Chews

One of the healthiest treats to give any dog is dental chews. While you will need to keep count of the treats as a part of your dog's daily caloric intake, they help with taking care of your dog's teeth. They aren't a replacement for

5 STEPS FOR BRUSHING YOUR PUGGLES TEETH

1. GET YOUR PUGGLE COMFORTABLE
Put a little toothpaste on your finger and let your Puggle sniff and lick it. Once they do, praise them for trying something new!

2. POSITION YOUR PUP FOR EASY CONTROL
In either an sitting or kneeling position, place your Puggle in between your legs with his head facing away from you. This will allow you to control him as he squirms at first.

3. BRUSH IN SMALL CIRCLES AROUND EACH TOOTH
After reapplying toothpaste to your finger, lift up your dog's upper lip, and begin to rub in circles around your Puggle's teeth. Your pup will likely make it difficult by constantly trying to lick your finger. Give your puppy praise when he doesn't wiggle too much. Try to move in a circular motion around each tooth, this will be hard with the smaller sharper teeth!

4. MASSAGE THE GUMS
Try to massage both the top and bottom gums. It is likely that the first few times you won't be able to do much more than get your finger in your dog's mouth, and that's okay. Over time, your puppy will learn to listen as training elsewhere helps your dog understand when you are giving commands

5. STAY POSITIVE
No, you probably won't be able to clean the puppy's teeth properly for a while, and that is perfectly fine so long as you keep working at it patiently and consistently.

regular brushing, but they are a good complement. Dogs tend to love these, and they help improve your dog's breath, so it is a win-win. Make sure to do your research to ensure that you are giving your dog the healthiest dental chews. You don't want to give your Puggle any treats that have questionable or uncertain ingredients.

CHAPTER 16
General Health Issues: Allergies, Parasites, and Vaccinations

Your Puggle will probably love the outdoors (especially if he takes after the Beagle side of the family), and with that comes a lot of risks. Environmental factors largely determine whether or not your dog gets parasites. For example, if you live near a wooded area, your dog is at a greater risk of having ticks than a dog that lives in the city. Fleas are a universal problem for all dogs because fleas can live in any grass, short or long. If you notice rashes or skin irritations, it could be an allergic reaction or symptoms of a parasite. Talk to your vet about all potential environmental risks and any skin conditions you notice when you groom your dog.

Photo Courtesy of Carole Robinson

CHAPTER 16   General Health Issues: Allergies, Parasites, and Vaccinations

The Role of Your Veterinarian

Scheduled veterinary visits, routine vaccinations, and regular checkups make for a healthy Puggle. If your dog seems sluggish or less excited than usual, it could be a sign there is something wrong with him. Fortunately, the breed's personality tends to make it easy to tell when your dog isn't feeling well. Annual visits to the vet will eliminate any problems that might be slowly draining the energy or the health from your dog.

Regular checkups also make sure that your Puggle is aging well. If your dog shows symptoms of a potential problem, an early diagnosis will address the problem. You and your vet can create a plan to manage any pain or problems that come with your dog's aging process. The vet may recommend adjustments to your schedule to accommodate your pup's aging body and his diminishing abilities. This will ensure that you can keep having fun together without hurting your dog.

Vets can provide treatment or preventive medication for parasites and other microscopic threats, which your dog might encounter on a daily basis. These attacks can happen when he is playing outside or when he is exposed to dogs or other animals.

> **HELPFUL TIP**
> **Skinfold Pyoderma**
>
> Puggles tend to have fewer skinfolds than their Pug parent, but if your Puggle inherited some of these adorable rolls, you'll want to keep an eye out for skinfold pyoderma. This condition is essentially a skin infection that develops in skinfolds on your dog. Symptoms of this condition include redness, foul odor, and discharge. If your dog develops skinfold pyoderma, speak to your vet about medicated washes. Antibiotics may also be prescribed.

Allergies

The scientific name for environmental allergies is atopic dermatitis. However, it is difficult to know if the problem is environmental or if it is a food you are feeding your dog.

The following symptoms can be seen when either type of allergy is present:
- Itching/scratching, particularly around the face
- Hot spots
- Ear infections
- Skin infections

- Runny eyes and nose (not as common)

Dogs often develop allergies when they are between one and five years old. Once they develop an allergy, canines never outgrow the problem. Dog allergies are usually a result of allergens (such as dust, mold, or pollen), which irritate the skin or nasal passage.

Photo Courtesy of Charlene Bemis

CHAPTER 16   General Health Issues: Allergies, Parasites, and Vaccinations

Since the symptoms are the same for food and environmental allergies, your vet will help determine the cause. If your dog has a food allergy, change the food that you give him. If he has an environmental allergy, he will need medication, just as humans do. There are several types of medications that can help your dog become less sensitive to allergens:

- Antibacterial/Antifungal – These treatments only address the problems that come with allergies; shampoos, pills, and creams usually do not directly treat the allergy itself.
- Anti-inflammatories – These are over-the-counter medications, which are comparable to allergy medicine for people. Don't give your dog any medication without first consulting with the vet. You will need to monitor your dog to see if he has any adverse effects. If your dog is lethargic, has diarrhea, or shows signs of dehydration, consult with your vet immediately.
- Immunotherapy – This is a series of shots that can help reduce your dog's sensitivity to whatever he is allergic to. You can learn from your vet how to give your dog these shots at home. Scientists are also developing an oral version of this medication to make it easier to take care of your dog.
- Topical – This medication tends to be a type of shampoo and conditioner that will remove any allergens from your dog's fur. Giving your dog a warm (not hot) bath can also help relieve itching.

To determine the best treatment for your situation, talk with your vet regarding available medications.

Inhalant and Environmental Allergies

Inhalant allergies are caused by things like dust, pollen, mold, and dog dander. Your dog might scratch at a particular hotspot, or he might paw at his eyes and ears. Some dogs have runny noses and sneeze prolifically, in addition to scratching.

Contact Allergies

Contact allergies mean that your dog has touched something that triggers an allergic reaction. Things like wool, chemicals in a flea treatment, and certain grasses can trigger irritation in a dog's skin, even causing discoloration. If left untreated, the allergic reaction can cause the affected area to emit a strong odor or cause fur loss.

Like food allergies, contact allergies are easy to treat because once you know what is irritating your dog's skin, you can remove the problem.

Fleas and Ticks

Make it a habit to check for ticks after every outing into the woods or near long grass or wild plants. Comb through your dog's fur and check his skin for signs of irritation and for any parasites. Since you will be doing this several times a week, you should be able to recognize when there's a change, such as a new bump.

Fleas are problematic because they're far more mobile than ticks. The best way to look for fleas is to make it a regular part of your brushing

Photo Courtesy of Jackie Cameron

CHAPTER 16   General Health Issues: Allergies, Parasites, and Vaccinations

sessions. If you see black specks on the flea comb after brushing through your dog's fur, this could be a sign of fleas.

Instead of using a comb, you can also put your dog on a white towel and run your hand over the fur. Fleas and flea dirt are likely to fall onto the towel. Fleas often are seen on the stomach, so you may notice them when your pup wants a belly rub. You can also look for behavioral indicators, such as incessant scratching and licking. If fleas are a problem, you will need to use flea preventative products on a regular basis once your puppy has reached the appropriate age.

Along with being annoying, both fleas and ticks can carry parasites and illnesses that can be passed on to you and your family. Ticks carry Lyme disease, which can be debilitating or deadly if untreated. Lyme disease symptoms include headaches, fever, and fatigue. The bite itself often has a red circle around it. Ticks will fall off your dog once they are full, so if you find a tick on your dog, it will either be looking for a place to latch onto your dog, or it will be feeding. Use the following steps to remove the tick if it has latched onto your dog.

1. Apply rubbing alcohol to the area where the tick is located.
2. Use tweezers to pull the tick off your dog. Do not use your fingers because infections are transmitted through blood, and you don't want the tick to latch onto you.
3. Place the tick in a bag and make sure it is secure so that it does not fall out. The vet can assess the type of tick for diagnostic purposes since different types of ticks carry different diseases.
4. Examine the spot where the tick was to make sure it is fully removed. Sometimes the head will remain under the dog's skin, so you will need to make sure all of the tick has been removed.
5. Set up a meeting with the vet to have your dog checked.

The FDA has issued a warning about some store-bought treatments for fleas and ticks. Treatments can be applied monthly, or you can purchase a collar for constant protection. Either way, make sure the treatment does not contain isoxazoline, which can have a negative effect on some pets. (This chemical is found in Bravecto, Nexgard, Credelio, and Simparica.)

Most ingredients in these treatments are safe if the proper dose is used. However, if you use a product that is meant for a larger dog, the effects can be toxic to your smaller dog. Consult your vet for recommended treatments and administer the appropriate dose of flea and tick repellant for your dog's size and needs. When you start applying the treatment, watch your dog for the following issues:

- Diarrhea/vomiting
- Trembling
- Lethargy
- Seizures

Take your dog to the vet if you notice any of these issues.

Never use any cat product on a dog and vice versa. If your dog is sick, pregnant, or nursing, you may need to look for an alternative preventative treatment. If you have a cat or young children, you should choose one of the other preventative options for keeping fleas and ticks away. This is because flea collars contain an ingredient that is lethal to felines and which might be carcinogenic to humans.

The packaging on flea treatments will advise you when to begin treating your dog based on his current age and size. Different brands have different recommendations, and you don't want to start treating your puppy too early. There are also important steps to applying the treatment. Make sure you understand all of the steps before purchasing the flea treatment.

If you want to use natural products instead of chemicals, research the alternatives and decide what works best for your Puggle. Verify that any natural products work before you buy them, and make sure you consult with your vet. Establish a regular monthly schedule and add it to your calendar so that you remember to consistently treat your dog for fleas and ticks.

Parasitic Worms

Although worms are a less common problem than fleas and ticks, they can be far more dangerous. The following lists the types of worms that you should be aware of:

- Heartworms
- Hookworms
- Roundworms
- Tapeworms
- Whipworms

Unfortunately, there isn't an easy-to-recognize set of symptoms to help identify when your dog has worms. However, you can keep an eye out for the following symptoms, and if your dog shows any of these warning signs, schedule a visit to the vet:

- Your Puggle is unexpectedly lethargic for at least a few days.

CHAPTER 16   General Health Issues: Allergies, Parasites, and Vaccinations

Photo Courtesy of Tawanda Harbison

- Patches of fur begin to fall out (this will be noticeable if you brush your Puggle regularly), or if you notice patchy spaces in your dog's coat.
- Your dog's stomach becomes distended (expands) and looks like a potbelly.
- Your Puggle begins coughing, vomiting, has diarrhea, or has a loss in appetite.

If you aren't sure about any symptom, it's always best to get your dog to the vet as soon as possible.

Heartworms

Heartworms are a significant threat to your dog's health and can be deadly as they can both slow and stop blood flow. As such, you should consistently treat your dog with heartworm protection.

Fortunately, there are medications that prevent your dog from developing heartworms. To prevent this deadly problem, you can give your dog a chewable medication, topical medicine, or you can request shots.

The heartworm parasite is carried by mosquitoes, which are nearly impossible to avoid in most regions of the country, and it is a condition that is costly and time-consuming to treat. Alleviating the disease is well worth the work in order to keep your pup healthy and happy.

The following are the steps involved in treating your dog for heartworms:
- The vet will draw blood for testing, which can cost as much as $1,000.
- Treatment will begin with some initial medications, including antibiotics and anti-inflammatory drugs.
- Following a month of the initial medication, your vet will give your dog three shots over the course of two months.

From the time of diagnosis until the confirmation your dog is free of heartworms, you will need to treat your Puggle very carefully. Caution is needed when you exercise your dog because the worms are in your dog's heart, and that inhibits blood flow. This means raising your dog's heart rate too much could kill him. Your vet will tell you how best to exercise your canine during this time. Considering your Puggle may be energetic, this could be a very rough time for both you and your dog.

Treatment will continue after the shots are complete. After approximately six months, your vet will conduct another blood test to ensure the worms are gone.

Once your dog is cleared of the parasites, you will need to begin medicating your dog against heartworms in the future. There will also be lasting damage to your dog's heart, so you will need to ensure that your dog does not over-exercise.

Intestinal Worms: Hookworms, Roundworms, Tapeworms, and Whipworms

All four of these worms thrive in your dog's intestinal tract, and they get there when your dog eats something contaminated with them. The following are the most common ways dogs ingest worms:
- Feces
- Small hosts, such as fleas, cockroaches, earthworms, and rodents
- Soil, including licking it from their fur and paws
- Contaminated water
- Mother's milk (If the mother has worms, she can pass them on to young puppies when they nurse.)

The following are the most common symptoms and problems caused by intestinal parasites:
- Anemia
- Blood loss
- Coughing
- Dehydration

CHAPTER 16 General Health Issues: Allergies, Parasites, and Vaccinations

- Diarrhea
- Large intestine inflammation
- Weight loss
- A pot-bellied appearance

If a dog lies in soil with **hookworm larvae,** the parasite can burrow through the canine's skin. Vets will conduct a diagnostic test to determine if your dog has this parasite, and if your dog does have hookworms, the vet will prescribe a de-wormer. If your dog is infested with hookworms, you should visit a doctor yourself because humans can get hookworms, too. Being treated at the same time as your Puggle will help stop the vicious cycle of continually trading off which of you has worms.

ROUNDWORMS

Roundworms are quite common, and at some point in their lives, most dogs have to be treated for them. The parasites primarily eat the digested food in your dog's stomach, getting the nutrients your dog needs. It is possible for larvae to remain in your dog's stomach even after all of the adult worms have been eradicated. If your Puggle is pregnant, her puppies should be checked periodically to make sure the inactive larvae are not passed on to the puppies. The mother will also need to go through the same testing to make sure the worms don't make her sick.

TAPEWORMS

Tapeworms are usually eaten when they are eggs and are usually carried by fleas or from the feces of other animals who also have tapeworms. The eggs develop in the canine's small intestine until they reach the adult stage. Over time, parts of the tapeworm will break off and can be seen in your dog's waste. If this happens, you should be very thorough when cleaning up any waste so other animals will not also contract tapeworms. While tapeworms are not usually fatal, they can cause weight loss and give your dog a potbelly. (The size of your dog's stomach depends on how big the worms grow in your dog's intestines.)

Your vet can test your dog for tapeworms and can prescribe medication to take care of the problem. The medication might include chewable tablets, regular tablets, or a powder that can be sprinkled on your dog's food. There is a minimal risk of humans catching tapeworms, but children are at the greatest risk. Be sure children wash their hands carefully if playing in areas used by your dog. It is also possible to contract tapeworms if a person swallows a flea, which is feasible if your dog and home have a serious infestation.

WHIPWORMS

Whipworms grow in the large intestine, and when in large numbers, they can be fatal. Their name is indicative of the appearance of their tails, which are thinner than their upper section. Like the other worms, you will need to have your dog tested to determine if he has acquired whipworms.

Staying current with flea treatments, properly disposing of your pet's waste, and making sure your Puggle does not eat trash or animal waste will help prevent your dog from getting these parasites.

Medication to prevent these four parasites can often be included in your dog's heartworm medication. Be sure to speak with your vet regarding the different options.

Vaccinating Your Puggle

Vaccination schedules are routine for most dog breeds, including Puggles. Make sure to add this information to your calendar, and until your puppy has completed his vaccinations, he should avoid contact with other dogs.

The following list can help you schedule your Puggle's vaccinations:

Timeline	Shot		
6 to 8 weeks	Bordetella Lyme	Leptospira Influenza Virus-H3N8	DHPP – First shot Influenza Virus-H3N2
10 to 12 weeks	Leptospira Lyme	DHPP – Second Rabies shot Influenza Virus-H3N8	Influenza Virus-H3N2
14 to 16 weeks	DHPP – Third shot		
Annually	Leptospira Lyme	Bordetella Influenza Virus-H3N8	Rabies Influenza Virus-H3N2
Every 3 Years	DHPP Booster	Rabies (if opted for longer duration vaccination)	

CHAPTER 16   General Health Issues: Allergies, Parasites, and Vaccinations

These shots protect your dog against a range of ailments. Keep in mind these shots should be a part of your dog's annual vet visit so you can continue to keep your pup safe!

Holistic Alternatives

Wanting to prevent exposure to chemical treatments for your dog makes sense, and there are many good reasons why people are moving to more holistic methods. However, if you decide to go with holistic medication, talk with your vet first about reputable options. You can also seek out Puggle experts for recommendations before you start trying any holistic methods of care.

It is possible something like massage therapy can help your dog, especially as he ages. Even chiropractic therapy is available for dogs, but you will need to be sure to find a reputable chiropractor for your pup, so the treatment doesn't do more harm than good, especially since Pugs can have issues with their spines. Follow recommendations on reputable, holistic Puggle websites to provide the best, safest care for your dog.

CHAPTER 17
Genetic Health Concerns Common to the Puggle

One of the biggest positive aspects of designer dogs is that they tend to have fewer health problems than purebred dogs. But just because the parents tend to have fewer health problems doesn't guarantee that your Puggle will be healthy. This is why it is vital to ensure that you find a breeder who tests their parent dogs and knows what their genetic history is. Chapter 4 details the recommended testing for both parent breeds.

Even the most careful breeder will occasionally have a puppy with a genetic ailment, no matter how careful they are about testing the parents and taking care of the mother during pregnancy. If you adopt an adult, you won't know as much about the Puggle's parents' genetic history.

Photo Courtesy of Eleonor Hughes

CHAPTER 17 Genetic Health Concerns Common to the Puggle

Common Pug Health Issues

Unfortunately, Pugs have a fairly high number of potential issues, in large part because of their adorable smooshed faces and wrinkles. The following are the kinds of issues you should monitor your Puggle for to ensure you can get help early on if it is needed.

Skin Issues

The wrinkles in their skin and propensity to have allergies tend to make Pugs have more sensitive skin than many other dogs. This is why Puggles should be brushed at least once a week – you are going to need to keep an eye out for a number of problems.

Demodectic Mange

If you see bald patches on your Puggle, it could be a sign of this particular type of mange. More commonly called Demodex, mites can make a home on your Puggle and cause the skin disease. Balding is the first symptom, with the first spot usually being about the size of a dime. It could be localized (largely just appearing in one place), or it could be all over the Puggle.

Vets often give dogs with Demodectic mange a series of dips that will kill the mites. This treatment can take up to three weeks and involve between 1 and 3 sessions, depending on the locations and severity of the mange. If the sessions do not work, your vet will talk to you about more serious treatments. It isn't likely that this will be necessary for a Puggle, but this is just one reason why monitoring your Puggle's skin regularly is important – you can prevent this kind of problem from getting too serious.

Skin Fold Pyoderma

Pyoderma occurs when bacteria accumulate in the skin folds (wrinkles). It tends to be at the worst around the face, lips, armpits, and groin. Obese dogs tend to have more problems with this as there are more wrinkles that are pressed tightly together. Keeping your dog at a healthy weight and regularly cleaning the skin folds with a damp (not wet) cloth tends to keep this from being a problem.

Allergies

If your Puggle is suffering from hot spots or if you notice his coat thinning during grooming sessions, watch for these other problems, which could be a sign of allergies:

- Wounds take longer to heal

- Weak immune system
- Aching joints
- Hair is falling out
- Ear infections

Regular brushing ensures that you are more aware of the state of your Puggle's coat, which can help you more quickly identify when your little dear is suffering from allergies. If you notice these issues, take your Puggle to the vet.

Brachial Issues

All dogs with incredibly short snouts suffer from a number of health problems because of those short noses. As covered in previous chapters, they are more prone to overheating, but that is not the only problem that they face.

Breathing

Brachial dogs are not able to breathe nearly as easily as dogs with medium to long snouts. It isn't just a matter of overheating; breathing is harder for them. As a result, it is nearly impossible for a dog with a nearly flat face to sneak up on anyone. You can hear him panting and snorting when he is in another room. It's kind of endearing, but it is also something that is beyond your dog's control.

When Puggles are eating or drinking, it tends to be a noisy occasion because their mouth is full, making it harder to get air at the same time. They are also notorious snorers, which is why you may not want to have them sleeping in the bed with you. Pugs also tend to drool while they sleep.

Some Pugs need corrective surgery when their condition is severe (if they have Brachycephalic Airway Syndrome, an elongated soft palate, or other problems associated with the short snouts), but it is incredibly unlikely that it will be an issue with your Puggle since the Beagle parent has a much longer snout. This often balances out to make surgery unnecessary for the mixed breeds.

Sneezing

Since Pugs often have allergies and breathing is a bit more difficult for them, they tend to sneeze a lot. It's just one more noisy activity you may need to get accustomed to if your Puggle has a flatter face. There isn't much you can do about this, but do be prepared for a bit of extra sneezing if your Puggle has allergies. It will also increase how much your Puggle drools.

CHAPTER 17 Genetic Health Concerns Common to the Puggle

Eye Problems

Brachial dogs tend to have more issues with their eyes than other breeds, both because of genetic problems and because of how far their eyes protrude, leaving them vulnerable to eye problems.

Cherry Eye

Glandular hypertrophy, better known as cherry eye, is caused by the third eyelid becoming inflamed. When this happens, you will be able to see the eyelid as it distends outward. Although it looks horrible, it is easily treated through surgery.

Corneal Problems

The cornea is the clear surface part of the eye, and it has three layers. When your dog gets a scratch, abrasion, or injury on the cornea, it can cause an ulcer. If untreated, this can lead to blindness. This is not a hereditary disease, but it is a common problem with brachial dogs because of the way their eyes protrude.

Photo Courtesy of Cara Park

Also, because the Pug's eyes protrude from their flat faces, that means that it is a lot easier to injure them. Pugs often end up having to get treated for scrapes and punctures to their corneas (the outer part of the eye that protects the more sensitive parts of the eye). When not properly treated, the injuries can get infected. Over time, this can affect the Pug's vision, including leading to blindness.

To protect his corneas, don't let your Puggle stick his head out of the window when you are driving. Watch for your Puggle scratching his eyes and for tearing up. If your pup is pawing his face often, take him to the vet to have his eyes checked.

Cataracts

Cataracts are a fairly common problem for all dogs as they age (as well as humans). Cataracts occur when the eye has a water imbalance or protein changes. If your dog's eyes appear to be cloudy, take him to the vet. If he's developing cataracts, your vet may have to remove them—cataracts can lead to blindness.

Ear Problems

Make sure you don't get water in your dog's ears. Puggles' floppy ears make it easier to trap moisture and bacteria, which is a really bad combination. If you monitor your Puggle's ears, you will likely avoid a majority of the problems with the ears.

Tail Problems

That cute curly Pug tail comes with a couple of potential problems. It isn't likely to be a problem for your Puggle, especially if your dog's tail takes after the Beagle parent, but you should be aware of what to watch for just in case.

Screw Tail

Screw tail is caused by malformed vertebrae in an animal's tail. This deformation can make the skin folds prone to infection, which can then affect how the animal goes to the bathroom. For dogs with this problem, there is usually a foul smell that will let you know your dog is having problems.

Treatment depends on the severity of the deformity. In the worst cases, surgery is required. For milder cases, vets may recommend nonsurgical treatments like regular washings with medicinal shampoo and antibiotics. It is not likely to be a problem with your Puggle, but you can have him checked by a vet to make sure his tail isn't deformed.

CHAPTER 17 Genetic Health Concerns Common to the Puggle

Limp Tail

Some dogs have a tail that remains limp, even when they are excited or interested – emotions that typically cause them to raise their tails. The problem could be caused by a deformity or an injury. If you catch your dog's tail in a door or if the tail is somehow injured, it could be broken or fractured. This will affect your dog's balance. In the event that an injury causes the problem, you will need to take your dog to the vet to have his tail set.

Stomach Issues

Pugs tend to have a number of stomach issues, largely because of the amount of air they swallow. You also need to be careful about the foods they eat – and this is why you should avoid giving them people food. The common problems are not typically severe, but it could mean that your Puggle will be more flatulent and may need to have his diet adjusted if you notice him farting more often or having softer stools.

Encephalitis

Encephalitis is a result of inflamed brain tissues and is seen most often in Pugs between two and three years old. It is a genetic issue, so it is more likely that your dog will have it if one or both of the parents did. It is a rare disease.

The primary symptom is seizures, which could be caused by a number of other issues. This means that the disease is often difficult to diagnose. It can cause other problems if it is not diagnosed. You will need to talk to your vet if you think this may be a problem. You should also contact the breeder to see if it is a problem for the parents. It may be a condition for which they will take the dog back.

Intervertebral Disk Disease

A problem common to dogs that are longer than they are tall, like the Pug and Beagle, intervertebral disk disease makes it more likely that the spinal disks will slip out of place, pressing against the spinal cord. As a result, the dog may suffer from muscle spasms, weaker limbs, demonstrate problems when walking, and be sensitive to the touch where the disk is out of place. Eventually, the condition can lead to paralysis if it goes untreated.

There are several treatments available, depending on the severity of the problem. Your vet can give you the best recommendation, ranging from medication to surgery. However, the problem is not entirely eliminated.

This is also one of the reasons why it is essential that you don't lift your dog off the ground. His long back means his lower half will move more when he is picked up off the ground, hurting his spine. Make sure that you and your family always follow the paws on the ground rule (Chapter 5).

Legg-Calve-Perthes Disease

Legg-Calve-Perthes disease is a degenerative bone disease that affects your dog's femurs. It is thought to be caused by a disruption in blood flow, which then weakens the bones. This can result in fractures and scarring to the surrounding tissue. One of the biggest concerns is that it typically leads to arthritis.

If your dog has this problem, you will notice limping of the affected leg. Touching the leg can be very painful for your dog, so you should go to the vet if you suspect your dog has this condition.

The disease is typically associated with smaller dogs, including Pugs. In this instance, your vet may recommend pain medication. Severe cases may require surgery.

Patellar Luxation

Pugs may suffer from patellar luxation, which involves slipping knee-caps. When the kneecaps are not properly fitted into the sockets, the back legs may have some minor problems. In most cases, patellar luxation is not a serious issue, and it is not known to cause much pain. However, occasionally it will require surgery to fix the repeated shift of the kneecap.

If your Puggle occasionally seems to be in pain when walking or cries when out running, this could be a sign of patellar luxation. Dogs tend to hold up the affected leg for a short period of time, trying to relieve the pain. It can be difficult to detect patellar luxation unless a dog has a more severe case, particularly as your dog ages. Treatment depends on the severity of the ailment. You should talk to your vet as a brace may be adequate for some dogs while others may require surgery.

Dental Issues – Small Mouths

Pugs have a number of dental issues that may be passed along to your Puggle, in large part because of their small mouths and short snouts. Breeding has made this breed more susceptible to gum disease. To ensure a healthy mouth, you should brush your dog's teeth on a regular basis (as covered in Chapter 15).

A Pug's teeth can break when playing with chew toys, and they may swallow the teeth, which can result in intestinal problems. You can give your Puggle safer chew toys (like Kongs and rope toys) and dental treats, but still, make sure you monitor while your Puggle chews on them.

CHAPTER 17 Genetic Health Concerns Common to the Puggle

Photo Courtesy of Marc and Erika Zachacki

Anal Glands

Anal glands produce a small amount of liquid every time your dog poops. Both male and female Pugs may have problems with these glands, including not fully emptying when the dog goes to the bathroom, which causes the glands to become enlarged. If you see your dog scooting across the floor on his rump or licking his backside a lot, it could be his attempt to fix the problem.

Over time, enlarged glands can be uncomfortable and can become infected. Vets aren't sure what causes this problem. Once it reaches this point, the vet will need to determine the right treatment, which includes surgery for the worst cases.

Obesity

As mentioned in previous chapters, Pugs are a breed that loves to eat. With their predisposition to joint problems, excess weight will slow them down earlier in their life and make it harder to walk. Obesity also increases the risk of other illnesses, like heart conditions.

Common Beagle Health Issues

Unfortunately, Beagles have just about as many health problems as Pugs because of their long breeding history. You will need to monitor your Puggle for all of these conditions to help make sure he remains healthy.

Dental Issues

Beagles are notorious for their dental issues. Tartar build-up can cause gum infections that can become more serious problems, like their teeth falling out. The plaque and tartar that is left to build up can be swallowed, where it will cause heart, joint, kidney, and liver damage.

Regularly brushing your dog's teeth (Chapter 15) is the easiest way to help keep your dog from having more severe dental problems.

Allergies

Beagles tend to have more environmental allergies than Pugs. Chapters 13, 15, and 16 cover symptoms and causes, but be aware that allergies are very much a problem for Beagles, so you should plan to monitor your dog for those issues.

CHAPTER 17   Genetic Health Concerns Common to the Puggle

Back Problems

Beagles are more likely to have intervertebral disc disease (IVDD) than many other breeds. IVDD is caused by the cushion between the vertebrae either rupturing or slipping, causing the disc to push on the spine. (Humans can also suffer from IVDD.) This problem is usually a result of overexertion or injuries.

Watch for your dog being reluctant to climb stairs, jump, or is having problems walking or going to the bathroom, and losing his appetite. He may also whimper or cry without any obvious problem or hunch his back and appear stiff when moving. In the most severe cases, he may not be able to use his back legs.

If you notice any of these problems, contact your vet immediately and set up an appointment. If your Puggle is unable to use his back legs, immediately go to an emergency vet clinic. Milder cases can be treated with medication. More severe cases often require surgery. If surgery is required, your dog will have the best results from the surgery if it is done within 24 hours of the symptoms appearing.

Eye Problems

Like Pugs, Beagles have a number of eye issues. In addition to watching for the problems common to Pugs' eyes, you'll need to monitor for these problems too.

Glaucoma

A painful eye ailment, glaucoma can result in blindness if it isn't treated early. If you notice your Puggle's eyes watering a lot, the cornea turning blue, or your dog squinting often, get him to the vet. These are signs that your dog is in pain.

You can have your vet do an annual glaucoma screening.

Distichiasis

Some Beagles have hairs that grow inside their eyelids, and those hairs rub against the cornea. It is a very painful problem that is more common in Beagles than nearly any other breed. It can cause corneal ulcers and other problems with the eyes.

If you notice your Puggle pawing at his eyes, this could be the problem. If diagnosed with distichiasis, the vet can easily treat it.

Hemophilia

Unfortunately, Beagles are prone to hemophilia, a disorder where their blood doesn't clot, so they will continue to bleed excessively, even from simple scratches. A test is required to determine if this is a problem for a dog, and it will affect the kinds of treatments that are available to your dog, including surgery.

You will need to be more careful about your dog getting injured, and any vet who sees your dog will need to know if this is a problem to provide the optimal treatment for other issues. For example, if your Puggle has hemophilia, surgery for a condition like cataracts may not be an option because it could be too risky for the dog.

Neurologic Issues

Beagles are more likely than most breeds to have neurological issues, including symptoms like tremors, seizures, and excessive sleeping. If you notice your Puggle exhibiting any of these issues, it is best to get him to the vet as quickly as possible to have him tested for a neurological disorder.

Liver Disorder

Some Beagles suffer from Copper Hepatopathy, a liver disorder. This disorder occurs when the dog's body creates toxic levels of copper that are stored in the liver. If not caught early, it can cause death.

If you notice your Puggle's eyes, gums, or skin looking yellowish, this is typically a sign of a liver disorder. It often shows up when a Beagle is between

> **HELPFUL TIP**
> **Identifying Canine Epilepsy**
>
> Puggles are typically a healthy breed, but, like any breed, they can be susceptible to several health conditions, one of which is canine epilepsy. Epilepsy affects around .75 percent of dogs and results from a brain abnormality that causes recurrent seizures. Identifying epilepsy can be tricky since seizures are caused by a variety of health issues. You can help your veterinarian diagnose your dog by providing video or detailed descriptions of your dog's seizures. The majority of epileptic canine seizures will happen suddenly, stop on their own, and last only a few seconds to minutes. During a seizure, be sure to stay calm and do not put anything into your dog's mouth. Most dogs are not in any pain during their seizures, and some are completely oblivious to them. There is no cure for epilepsy, but symptoms may be managed with medication and/or therapy.

CHAPTER 17   Genetic Health Concerns Common to the Puggle

two and four years old. You can have your Puggle scanned for it even if he doesn't have symptoms to make sure that it won't be a problem as he ages.

Heart Disease

Beagles are prone to many types of heart disease, both when they are young and when they are older. Your vet needs to make sure to regularly listen for any potential heart problems, such as palpitations or irregular rhythms. It is recommended that Beagles have annual heart checks to make sure their heart is healthy. It may be a good idea to do the same for your Puggle.

Cushing's Disease

The scientific name of this disease is Hyperadrenocorticism, and it occurs when the adrenal glands start to malfunction. As a result of this malfunction, your dog's body overproduces steroid hormones. The symptoms start to show early, but they are easy to miss because they appear to be minor issues.

Symptoms include your dog drinking more frequently and being hungrier than usual, while being less active. These symptoms can be difficult to detect since you are less likely to notice them. However, as the problem progresses, your Puggle may have a potbelly, develop thinner skin, and start to lose hair.

If your dog has Cushing's Disease, the vet will prescribe medication, and you will need to regularly monitor the condition. Initially, it will take close work with your vet to make sure the right dose of medication is determined.

Hip Dysplasia

Dysplasia is a result of the dog's hip and leg sockets being malformed, and that often leads to arthritis as the improper fit damages cartilage. The condition is possible to detect by the time a dog becomes an adult. The only way to detect it is through X-rays.

This is a problem that your Puggle may try to hide because he won't want to slow down. Your dog will walk a little more stiffly or may pant even when it's not hot. The condition usually becomes more obvious as a dog nears his golden years. Similar to the way older people tend to change their gait to accommodate pain, your dog may do the same. Getting up might be a little more difficult in the beginning and will likely get worse as he ages.

While surgery is an option in severe cases, most dogs can benefit from less invasive treatments:

- Anti-inflammatory medications – talk to your vet (dogs should not have large doses of anti-inflammatory drugs on a daily basis the way people do since aspirin and anti-inflammatories can damage your dog's kidneys)
- Lower the amount of high impact exercise your dog gets, especially on wood floors, tile, concrete, or other hard surfaces
- Joint fluid modifiers
- Physical therapy
- Weight loss (for dogs who are overweight or obese)

Photo Courtesy of Lori Agnello

CHAPTER 17 Genetic Health Concerns Common to the Puggle

Amyloidosis

Beagles are more likely to suffer from Amyloidosis than many other breeds. This ailment is the result of proteins in the body being altered so that they are deposited in places where they shouldn't be, like the liver, kidneys, and pancreas, where it will cause other problems within those organs. It can also affect the skin, causing a high fever.

Watch your dog for a loss of appetite, an increased need to go to the bathroom, greater thirst, diarrhea, vomiting, and loss of weight. The condition is more likely to start when a dog is young. The only treatment is managing your dog's appetite and fever (if he has one), and that can improve his life.

Obesity

Just like the Pug, obesity is a problem for Beagles. This is why it is especially important to be careful of how much you feed your Puggle – there is an incredibly high chance of your dog overeating and gaining too much weight.

Common Owner Mistakes

In addition to genetic problems, there are things you can do that could unintentionally damage your dog's health; these mistakes are related to diet and exercise levels. In the puppy stage, it is a difficult balance to strike as your puppy is curious and enthusiastic. Even when he is a fully grown dog, you have to make sure you are minimizing how much stress is placed on your Puggle's body. Weight management is one important way of keeping your dog healthy. You need to balance your dog's diet with his level of activity to prevent exacerbation of hip and elbow dysplasia.

Failing to notice early signs of potential issues can be detrimental, even fatal to your Puggle. With two parent breeds that have numerous health problems, any changes in your Puggle's behavior is likely a sign of something that should be checked by your vet.

Prevention and Monitoring

A Puggle may be cute when he is overweight, but an unhealthy habit of overfeeding can cause severe damage to his health. Take extra time to exercise with your dog, a habit that is healthy and fun for both of you!

Checking your Puggle's weight is important and should be done at least once a quarter or twice a year. You and your vet should keep an eye on your dog's weight; being overweight puts a strain on your dog's back, legs, joints, and muscles.

CHAPTER 18
The Aging Puggle

Since this designer breed has been around for a few decades, Puggles' life expectancy is more certain than many other designer dogs. Most Puggles live between 10 and 15 years, giving you over a decade of joy and companionship. Still, that probably won't feel like nearly long enough.

If you take really good care of your Puggle, keeping him from overindulging in food and regularly taking him to the vet, your pup will live longer. This makes it all the more important to make sure your pup gets regular exercise and has a good diet.

Puggles are considered seniors when they are between 6 and 8 years old. By the time your Puggle reaches 8, you will notice that your Puggle doesn't have quite as much energy and will probably walk a little more stiffly than in previous years. A dog may remain healthy his whole life, but as the years start to take their toll, his body may not be able to enjoy the same activities.

The first signs of aging usually appear as stiffness in his gait or heavy panting that begins early in your walk. If you see these changes, start to cut back on the long walks and go for shorter ones more often. Your Puggle may want to continue to be active, which calls for an adjustment in his activities but not a complete stop.

Be sure your pup doesn't overexert himself if he tries to remain active. Your Puggle may not want to accept the fact that things are changing. Fortunately for your Puggle, he will usually remain fairly happy as long as he is able to just lounge with you—it's one of the major benefits to have such an affable dog. He is always happy just being with his family, so he isn't going to be nearly so upset about losing his ability to be as active as many other breeds.

There is a reason this period of time is called the Golden Years…you can relax and enjoy this time of your dog's life as well. You don't have to worry about him tearing up things because he's bored or becoming over excited when seeing a squirrel during his walks. Instead, you can enjoy lazy evenings, peaceful weekends, and less-strenuous exercise. It's easy to make the senior years incredibly enjoyable for your Puggle and yourself by making the necessary adjustments.

CHAPTER 18 The Aging Puggle

Photo Courtesy of Joseph Barilla

Senior Care Challenges – Common Physical Disorders Related to Aging

Accommodations you should make for your senior Puggle include:

- Set water bowls in a couple of different places so that your dog can reach them easily.
- Cover hard floor surfaces (such as tile, hardwood, and vinyl) with non-slip carpets or rugs.
- Use cushions and softer bedding for your Puggle to make things more comfortable. There are even bed warmers for dogs if your Puggle displays achy joints or muscles. You also need to make sure he isn't too warm, so this can be a fine balancing act.
- To improve his circulation, increase how often you brush your Puggle.
- Keep your dog inside in extreme heat or cold. An old canine cannot handle changes in temperature as well as he once did.
- Use stairs or ramps so that your old pup doesn't have to do any jumping.
- Avoid moving furniture around in your home, particularly if your Puggle shows signs of problems with his eyesight or if he has dementia. A familiar home is more comforting and less stressful for your pet as he ages. If your Puggle isn't able to see as clearly as he once did, you should make sure his surroundings remain familiar to him, which will make it easier for him to move around without hurting himself.
- Consider setting up an area for your dog that allows him to avoid stairs, especially if climbing seems to bother him.
- Create a space with fewer distractions and noises where your Puggle can relax. Don't make your old friend feel isolated; instead, give him a place where he can get away from everyone if he needs to be alone.
- Be prepared to let your dog go outside for restroom breaks more often.

Previous chapters address illnesses that are common in a Puggle. However, old age tends to bring a slew of ailments that are not particular to any one breed. Here are other things you will need to watch for (as well as talking to your vet about if they occur):

- Arthritis is probably the most common ailment in any dog breed, and the Puggle is no exception. If your dog is experiencing stiffness and pain after normal activities, talk with your vet about ways to help minimize your Puggle's discomfort.
- Gum disease is a common issue in older dogs as well, and you should continue brushing your dog's teeth on a regular basis as he ages. A

CHAPTER 18 The Aging Puggle

regular check of your Puggle's teeth and gums can help ensure no problem develops.

- Loss of eyesight or blindness is relatively common in older dogs, just as it is in humans. Have your dog's vision checked at least once a year or more often if it is obvious his eyesight is failing.
- Kidney disease is a frequent problem in older dogs and one that you should watch for as your Puggle ages. If your canine drinks a lot of water and has accidents frequently, take him to the vet as soon as possible and have him checked for kidney disease.
- Although diabetes is usually thought of as a genetic condition, any Puggle can become diabetic if not fed and exercised properly. This is another reason why it's so important to be careful with your Puggle's diet and exercise levels.

Photo Courtesy of Anne Venet

Vet Visits – The Importance of Regular Vet Visits and What to Expect

As your Puggle ages, slowing down and occasional pain will become obvious. If your Puggle has a debilitating ailment or condition, discuss options for giving him a better quality of life. For example, wheelchairs are available if your Puggle shows problems with mobility.

Just as humans visit the doctor more often as they age, you'll need to take your dog to see your vet with greater frequency, too. The vet can make sure your Puggle stays active without overdoing it, and he can help alleviate unnecessary stress in your dog's life.

Based on your Puggle's changing personality and physical abilities, your vet might recommend changes to your dog's daily schedule and to his typical activities to keep your Puggle happy and active during the later years.

The following are the kinds of things to expect when you go to the vet:

- Your vet is going to talk about your dog's history even if you have visited every year. This talk is necessary to see how your dog's life has changed over time and to pinpoint when problems manifested themselves or got worse.
- Your vet will probably conduct a complete physical examination to assess your dog's current health.
- Depending on your dog's age and on his health, your vet may want to run some tests. The following are some of the most common tests for older dogs:
    - Arthropod-borne disease testing, which involves drawing blood and testing it for viral infections
    - Chemistry screening for kidney, liver, and sugar evaluation
    - Complete blood count
    - Fecal flotation, which involves mixing your dog's poop with a special liquid to test for worms and other parasites
    - Heartworm testing
    - Urinalysis, which tests your dog's urine to check the health of his kidneys and urinary system
- Routine wellness check, which the vet has been conducting on your dog for years.
- Any breed-specific tests for your aging Puggle.

CHAPTER 18 The Aging Puggle

Changes That Might Occur

Keep an eye out for different signs that your dog is slowing down. This will help you to know when to adjust the setup around your home and to reduce how much your old pup is exercising.

Appetite and Nutritional Requirements

With less exercise, your dog won't need as many calories as usual, which means you will need to adjust his diet. If you opted to feed your Puggle

Photo Courtesy of Alexandra Olsen

commercial dog food, make sure to now change to a senior dog formula. Senior food is designed for the changing dietary needs of older dogs by including fewer calories and adding more nutrients.

If you prepare dog food at home, talk to your vet and research how best to reduce calories without sacrificing taste. Your canine is going to need less fat in his diet, so you should make healthier food choices while still considering the taste. These dietary changes will certainly be different from the puppy and active adult foods you fed your Puggle in the past.

Exercise

It's up to you to adjust your dog's schedule and to keep him less active yet happy. Shorter and more frequent walks should take care of your Puggle's exercise needs, as well as helping to break up your day a little more.

Your dog will enjoy napping as much as walking, especially if he gets to cuddle with you. Sleeping beside you while you watch television or as you nap is pretty much all it takes to make your older Puggle content!

You may notice your Puggle spends more time sniffing during walks, which could be a sign that your dog is tiring. If he is walking slower, looking up at you, and flopping down, that could be his way of letting you know it's time to return home. If your canine can no longer manage long walks, make them shorter and more often. You could also spend more time romping around your yard or at home with your buddy.

Photo Courtesy of Angel Torres

CHAPTER 18   The Aging Puggle

Aging and the Senses

Just like people, dogs' senses weaken as they get older. They won't hear things as well as they used to, they won't see things as clearly, and their sense of smell will weaken.

The following are some of the signs your dog is losing at least one of his senses:

- It becomes easy to surprise or startle your dog. You need to be careful because this can make your Puggle aggressive.
- Your dog may seem to ignore you or is less responsive when you issue a command.
- Cloudy eyes may be a sign of sight loss, though it does not mean your dog is blind.

If your aging dog seems to "behave badly," it is a sign that he is aging, not that he wants to rebel. Do not punish your older dog.

Adjust your schedule to meet your dog's changing abilities. Adjust his water bowl's height, refrain from rearranging rooms, and pet your dog more often. Make sure his bed is fluffy, or get him a new, more comfortable bed. Put the bed on the floor if it was previously kept on furniture. Your dog is probably nervous about losing his abilities, so it is up to you to comfort him.

Keeping Your Senior Dog Mentally Active

Just because your older Puggle can't walk as far as he used to doesn't mean his brain is weaker too. As long as your Puggle performs all of the basic commands, you can teach him all kinds of new, low-impact tricks.

At this point, training could be easier because your Puggle has learned to focus better, and he'll be happy to have something he can still do with you. New toys are another fun way to help keep your dog's mind active. Be careful the toys aren't too rough on your dog's jaw and teeth. There are also food balls, puzzles, and other games that focus on cognitive abilities...and games such as hide and seek will still be very much appreciated!

Some senior dogs suffer from cognitive dysfunction syndrome (CCD), a type of dementia. It is estimated that 85% of all cases of dementia in dogs go undiagnosed because of the difficulty in pinpointing the problem. It manifests itself more as a problem of temperament than of cognitive ability.

If your dog begins to act differently, you should take him to the vet to see if he has CCD. While there really isn't any treatment for this problem, your vet can recommend things that will help your dog focus. An action such as rearranging the furniture is strongly discouraged because your dog relies on the familiarity of his surroundings to reduce his stress.

Mental stimulation at this time of your Puggle's life is also still a must. Not only will keeping his mind active fight CCD, but it will also keep him healthy whether he exhibits signs of dementia or not.

Advantages to the Senior Years

The last years of your Puggle's life can be just as enjoyable (if not more so) than the earlier stages since your dog has mellowed over time. All those high-energy activities will give way to relaxing and enjoying time with you. Your Puggle will continue to be a loving companion, interacting with you at every opportunity. That does not change with age. However, your canine's limitations should dictate interactions and activities. If you are busy, make sure you schedule time with your Puggle to do things that are within those limitations. It is just as easy to make an older Puggle happy as it is to make a young dog happy!

Preparing to Say Goodbye

No pet parent wants to think about this last step, but as you watch your Puggle slow down, you will know when your time with your sweet pup is coming to an end. Some dogs can continue to live for years after they begin to slow down, but many dogs don't make it more than a year or two. Sometimes dogs will lose their interest in eating, will have a stroke, or another problem will arise without warning. Eventually, it will be time to say goodbye, whether at home or at the vet's office. You need to be prepared.

Talk to your family about how you should care for your dog over the last few years or months of his life. Many dogs will be perfectly happy, continuing life as usual, despite their limited abilities. Some may begin to have problems controlling their bowel movements, while others may have problems getting up from a prone position. There are solutions to all of these problems. Always remember that quality of life should be your primary concern. Since your

> **FUN FACT**
> **Oldest Beagle**
>
> A Puggle has yet to make history for its longevity, but a Beagle, one half of your Puggle's genetic makeup, lived an impressive 28 years. Butch, a Beagle from the USA, was born in 1975 and passed away in 2003. A Puggle's typical lifespan is about 10-15 years on average.

CHAPTER 18 The Aging Puggle

dog cannot tell you how he feels, you must take cues from your Puggle. If your dog still seems happy, there is no reason to have him euthanized.

At this stage, your dog is probably happy just sleeping near you for eighteen hours a day. This is perfectly fine as long as he still gets excited about walking, eating, and being petted. The purpose of euthanasia is to reduce suffering, not to make things more convenient for yourself. This is what makes the decision so difficult, but your dog's behavior should be a fairly good indicator of how he is feeling. Here are some other things to watch when evaluating your dog's quality of life:

- Appetite
- Drinking
- Urinating and defecation
- Pain (noted by excessive panting)
- Stress levels
- Desire to be active or with family (If your dog wants to be alone most of the time, this is usually a sign he is trying to be alone for the end of his life.)

Talk to your vet if your dog has a serious illness to determine the best path forward. They can provide the best information on the quality of your dog's life and how long your dog is likely to live with his disease or ailment.

If your dog gets to the point where he is no longer happy, he can't move around, or he has a fatal illness, it is probably time to say goodbye. This is a decision that should be made as a family, always putting the dog's needs and quality of life first. If you decide it is time to say goodbye, determine who will be present at the end.

If you have decided to euthanize your dog, you can make his last few minutes calming and peaceful by feeding your dog the things he couldn't eat before. Foods like chocolate and grapes can put a smile on his face for his remaining time in your life.

You can also have your dog euthanized at home. If you decide to request a vet to come to your home, be prepared for additional charges for the home visit. You also need to determine where you want your dog to be, whether inside or outside, and in which room if you decide to do it inside.

Make sure at least one person he knows well is present so that your dog is not alone during the last few minutes of his life. You don't want your dog to die surrounded by strangers. The process is fairly peaceful, but your dog will probably be a little stressed. He will pass within a few minutes of the injection but continue to talk to him as his brain will continue to work even after his eyes close.

Once your dog is gone, you need to determine what to do with the body:

- Cremation is one of the most common ways of taking care of the body. You can request an urn or ask for a container for his ashes so you can scatter your dog's ashes over his favorite places. Make sure you don't spread his ashes in places where this action is not permitted. Private cremation is more expensive than communal cremation, but it means the only ashes you receive are from your dog. Communal cremation occurs when several pets are cremated together.

- Burial is the easiest method after your dog is euthanized and can be performed at your home. However, you need to check local regulations to be sure burying your dog on your property is legal. You also need to consider the soil; if your yard is rocky or sandy, that will create problems when trying to bury your pet. Also, don't bury your pet in a spot that is near a well that people use as a drinking source or if it is near wetlands or waterways. Your dog's body can contaminate the water as it decays. You can also look into a pet cemetery if there is one in your area.

Grief and Healing

Dogs become members of our families, so their passing can be incredibly difficult. People go through all of the same emotions and feelings of loss with a dog as they do with close friends and family. The absence of your dog's presence in your life is jarring, especially with such a loving, loyal dog like the Puggle. It will feel weird not to have that presence by your side as you move around your home, and it will be a constant reminder of your loss. In the beginning, you and your family will probably feel considerable grief. Saying goodbye will be extremely difficult, so taking a couple of days off work is not a bad idea. While some people might say your Puggle was "just a dog," you know better; it is okay to feel the pain and to grieve as you would for any lost loved one.

Losing your Puggle is also going to create a substantial change in your schedule. It will likely take a while to become accustomed to the shift in your day-to-day life. Fight the urge to go out and get a new dog because you almost certainly will not be ready yet.

Everyone grieves differently, so allow yourself to grieve in a way that is healthy for you. Everyone in your family will feel the loss differently, too, so let them do the same. Some people don't require much time, while others can feel the loss for months. There is no timetable, so don't try to force it on yourself or on any member of your family.

CHAPTER 18 The Aging Puggle

Talk about how you would like to remember your pup. You can have a memorial for your lost pet, tell stories, or plant a tree in your dog's memory.

Try to return to your normal routine as much as possible if you have other pets. This can be both painful and helpful as your other pets will still need you just as much as when your Puggle was alive. This is especially true of other dogs that have also lost their companion.

If you find grief is hindering your ability to function normally, seek professional help. If needed, you can search online to find support groups in your area to help you and your family, especially if this was your first dog. Sometimes it helps to talk about the loss so that you can begin to heal.

www.ingramcontent.com/pod-product-compliance
Lightning Source LLC
Chambersburg PA
CBHW071445070526
44578CB00001B/215